The Mancunian Hero

The Mancunian Hero

Catherine J.M. Hughes

ISBN:	Softcover	978-1-9845-9287-3
	eBook	978-1-9845-9286-6

Print information available on the last page.

Rev. date: 12/02/2019

To order additional copies of this book, contact:
Xlibris
800-056-3182
www.Xlibrispublishing.co.uk
Orders@Xlibrispublishing.co.uk
806534

CONTENTS

FOREWORD

The picture on the front cover is Norman Leslie Moors when he was twenty one, taken in Gibraltar.

This story is about a Royal Navy Hero, Norman Leslie Moors and in memory of him. My Uncle, who said to me:

"Being in the Royal Navy was very hard working and often nerve racking, but interesting and enjoyable.

"Swinging the lamp" or "shooting a line" are naval terms for telling a story. But this one is true.

I also want Catherine, to write about things I feel very strongly about, injustices, politics, religion, trade unionism, poverty, class distinction, royalty, the world, greed, selfishness. Those last two are two of the biggest sins which cause most of the world's troubles. As Ghandi says, "There is enough for every man's needs but not enough for every man's greed's." I have asked my niece Catherine Jean Mary Hughes, to write this book and have it published in memory of me and I thank her for her valuable work she has done in producing this book."

By Catherine J.M. Hughes

The Rodney Association Cub Badge.

(Eagles do not breed doves).

(Eagles do not breed doves).

ASSOCIATION

Membership No. ...324......

Name ....N.L. Moors..................

Address .16 Camden Road,..........

...Layton,......................

...BLACKPOOL...FY3 8HN...

....

~~Rank on leaving ship~~ ....

DEDICATION

I dedicate this book;
"The Mancunian Hero."
In Honour of My Uncle.
My Mother's brother. Norman Leslie Moors.
After a long hard service in the Royal Navy, He
was a Hero and he had a happy life.
He died on 21st January 2015 aged 92.
And I thank him for the stories;
he contributed to in the writing of this book.

ACKNOWLEDGEMENTS

I wish to give a huge thank you to Peter and Josephine Cropper for their care and patience in editing this book.

CHAPTER 1

Twins Are Born

In the year 1922 on December 4th twin boys were born to Mary Moors and Henry Atkinson Moors. at number 3 Cornbrook Park Road, Old Trafford, Stretford. On the border of Manchester, Hulme district. St Georges Park was at the rear of the house. Most people in that area knew the park as "Barracks Park", as it was a cavalry barracks in the 1914-1918 war. The house was the end one of a row of five. It was a double bay front house. The bottom of the house was used as a small printing works, owned by Mr Henry Atkinson Moors, the father of the twin boys. The upper part of the house consisted of first floor, kitchen, bathroom (no hot water), living room, their Mum and Dad's bedroom. Then there was the second floor, attic, large landing, two bedrooms (one for the boys, one for the girls) and a small box room for junk.

The only window in the boys' room was in the roof. In the room was one iron double bed, one iron single bed. Norman and George slept together. David slept in the single one. There were large tin trunks to keep clothes in. There was nothing else, except a fireplace. The girls' room comprised of one double bed, one large dresser with a lot of drawers.

The family consisted of three girls and four boys. In order of age the girls were Dora, Hilda, Edna, and the boys were David, George, Norman and Noel.

Dora left home to live with her Grandma Moors when Norman was only a small boy. David the eldest son worked for his Dad, also

Hilda the middle daughter worked for her Dad. David worked the printing machines and as the compositor. Hilda did the book binding and numbering. There was a guillotine to cut stacks of paper. Only their Dad worked that. He cut his finger off, with it, at the first joint, the one next to his thumb on his right hand. He ran the business side of things and did gold blocking. The machines were run from a gas engine, which was in the cellar. There was a belt drive off the gas engine flywheel, and up to the floor above, via shafting and belts to the machines. He also put a generator on the cellar floor. This was driven off the shafting by a belt, for low voltage lighting when working the machines, as the lighting was only gas in all the building. The Moors printing firm was four generations old, David being the fourth generation. "Henry A Moors & Son". A neighbour, one day, seeing their Mum with two baby boys in the pram, asked her if she would name one of the boys after her baby boy who had died. She said she would, Leslie being that name. His Mum registered the twins, Noel and Leslie. Later when their Dad found out he disagreed, and wanted Leslie, to be called Norman.

So the twins were christened Norman and Noel. From then on, it was Norman and Noel. Noel died at six months old and Norman grew up not knowing he was a twin. Until he was fourteen and needed his birth certificate to take to the Employment Dept. so he could leave school and start work. His Mum gave him his birth certificate, which had the name Leslie Moors on. So he said, "Who is this? It's not mine." She said "It's yours. ". he said, "It's not, this has Leslie Moors on, and my name is Norman." She said, "I will have to tell you now, all about it."

As a small child Norman played in the back garden with his sister Edna who was two and a half years older. She also took him to school, when he was four and a half, she was seven. The school was a long way two or three miles. It was Seymour Park infants and juniors, at the end of Northumberland Road near Ayres Road. Norman went home for dinner and back to school then home at 4pm. He was falling asleep on the way home. (No school dinners or free milk in those days.)

As a small boy Norman used to kneel on a chair watching the horses and carts going up and down Cornbrook Park Road. The men used to have sacks on their heads and shoulders when it was raining. Some were cruel, and whipped the horses which were pulling heavy loads. The horses had to have sacking on their hooves in winter to stop them slipping. The shire horses were big and strong. For some heavy loads, four horses were needed.

As Norman grew older and was able to go out on his own, he went looking at Pomona Docks where the banana and Guinness boats came in from the Manchester Ship Canal. All sorts of insects and large spiders came off these boats. One time when Edna and Norman were playing in the back garden where there were two trees, a low wall, and the trees and bushes of St Georges Park. A large spider jumped off the wall, and ran towards them both. They ran into the house and shut and bolted the back door. His Mum said "What are you bolting the door for?" "It's a big spider after us!". They explained. "Nonsense." Mum said, but she looked through the window and saw the big spider on the doorstep. So they had to wait until it went away. Norman also went into Salford across the River Irwell via Mark Addy Bridge and Hulme Hall Road, to play in Ordsall Park where they had plenty of swings and roundabouts. The River Irwell was very dirty, with all the factories dumping their dirty waste in it. He also used to go to Trafford Bridge, which was a swing bridge. It was a road bridge that had to swing round to let the big ships go past on the ship canal. His Mum used to take them to Peel Park in Salford some Sunday afternoons. They also used to visit relatives in Latchford and Bolton.

When Norman was about eight, he went to learn to swim with his brother George who was five years older than him. They went to Northumberland Road Baths and taught themselves to swim. When Norman was older he could swim but couldn't dive. He was kidding his pals that he could dive, until one day he was at the baths on his own, when some of them came into the baths, they couldn't dive either. Norman was standing on the side of the pool at the four foot, six inch in depth. When they asked him to show them that he could dive, he wasn't going to back down, so he dived in. They said "That was good, how did you learn to do it?" Norman said "That's the first time he have dived!". They wouldn't believe him. They had nick names. Normans' was 'Mo' - short for Moors.

Sometimes in the summer holidays they used to go to Dunham Park in Cheshire where there were deer. It was a long way right down Chester Road. His Mum used to give them big bottles of water and doorstep sandwiches. George, Edna and Norman used to go out all day and, had soon eaten the sandwiches and were still hungry. So, they went in the fields gathering raw potatoes, turnips, carrots and anything they could find. George had to carry Norman on his back on the way home as he was fast asleep. When Norman got older he would go off with his own pals to Longford Park in Stretford, and also to the clay pits in that area. He got very dirty and his clothes got in a mess going to the clay pits. His Dad said, "Clay pits! Out of bounds." However he loved playing in the clay pits as they had corrugated iron sheets to sit on and slide down the slopes of the big pits. Some got full of water so the lads made rafts. Sometimes, some lads fell off the rafts and couldn't swim and drowned. The lads also used to swim in the canal at Stretford near the River Mersey. The water was dirty and they had to dry themselves on their shirts.

On the way home from clay pits, they used to stop at the horse trough to clean up, Norman only had a hanky, so he was still in a mess when he got home. His dad saw the mess he was in, and knew he had been to the clay pits again. "Upstairs you." He would say. "No tea for you and you will stay there till morning. he will be up in a bit." "Don't you dare give him anything mother! ". Norman would get under the iron double bed, and his dad, would get hold of the bed at the side and ram it against the wall, so Norman had no way out. He would grab Norman from under the bed and throw him on top of it. His dad had a big leather belt, and he gave Norman a good beating with it. Norman had many of them, so as time went by he got used to the pain. He soon stopped crying after he had gone down stairs. His dad, noticed this and came back, saying, "Stopped crying have you? You've not had enough! ". Then he gave him some more. Norman used to have to carry on crying for a while so his dad wouldn't come back. When Norman went out playing with other boys, sometimes they had fights. They couldn't hurt Norman as much as his dad could, so he won most of the fights.

Norman used to have to go to church on Sunday mornings with his sister Edna; They went to the Albert Hall Methodist Church on Peter Street in the morning, and Sunday school in the afternoon. At that time he didn't know or notice that Edna was brain damaged. His dad did that. He caused it by hitting Norman's mum while she was pregnant. Edna had a very strong voice and liked singing. She could have made it as an opera singer. When the Sunday school children gave a show from time to time. at the Albert Hall which was a very big place, she would be on one side with the girls, and Norman would be on the other side with the boys. He had to sing solo, the same as she did. He didn't like it but she did. She would sing a few lines then he would sing a few lines, each, in turn, until the hymn was finished.

Later Norman joined the Boys Brigade, which was nearer home. He was in the band, blowing a bugle. He went every night doing drill, games, crafts and band practice, he also went camping with the Manchester battalion of all Boys' Brigades within Manchester. There were about one hundred boys in his brigade, the Ninth Manchester's, which was based at Tatton Street Mission, Hulme district. One year they won the colours, that is, the standard flags of the Boy's Brigade. To win it you have to be the smartest and best at drill. The drill test was done at the territorial drill hall at All Saints. A sergeant major did the drilling. When going to camp for a fortnight in Wales, the brigade that had won the colours led the Battalion as well as any big parade for that year.

He enjoyed going round the streets with the Boys Brigade in the band blowing a bugle on a Sunday morning, waking all the people up. He practised blowing bugle in the back garden with three other boys. The neighbours complained when blowing the Last Post, as it reminded them of lost ones during the 1914 - 1918 war. His dad said we must practise in the cellar. They did and all was well. The Boys Brigade motto was "Sure and Steadfast". Norman joined the YMCA juniors at thirteen. His brother George joined the seniors, he was eighteen. There was a gym with instructors. It had a running track above, which ran right around the gym. Next to it was a swimming baths. There was a large room full of table tennis tables and another one full of billiard tables. There was a cinema, a cafe and rooms to read in. It was ten shillings a year for juniors and one pound a year for seniors. Norman enjoyed playing there, it was great.

Norman was football mad, but couldn't kick with his left foot, so he had to try harder and harder, he stopped kicking with his right foot and only with his left until he could kick with both feet.

They had very little money to spend, so made their own fun. They used paper balls or rag balls for a football. If one boy had a ball it would only be a small one. They often used a tennis ball, they played in the street using a lamppost as wickets or even goalposts. Police used to shift them, telling them to go in the park. The park was St Georges and the pitches were red shale, goalposts made of steel tubes. When you fell you cut all your knees. Tennis courts were red shale also. There was a gym, two bowling greens, and a paddling pool and swimming baths, which were three foot to eight foot deep. There were no changing rooms then, just a long form, with a roof over. So, you had to keep one eye on your clothes to prevent them being pinched and they used to swim in cold water. His brother David was very good at making kites. He made Norman one out of brown paper, some string and long thin bits of wood.

He had cut it with a penknife. It would fly so high it was lost in the clouds. Norman used to tie it to a form and go and play football. The park keeper used to say "Come on lads, get those kites in. The park is closing in half an hour."

One day when Norman was in junior school, instead of going home for his dinner he went to Seymour Park with his pal Martin Bonus to play on the swings and in the sand pit. It had a lot of rainwater in it. They hadn't noticed the time passing by until they saw the children going back to school. They hadn't been home for dinner. Norman ran home, his dad was there in the print works, and he saw him. He said, "Upstairs you! No dinner or tea. You will stay there 'till next morning." He gave Norman a good hiding as well.

One day Norman had to go for some milk at the grocer's at the top end of Cornbrook Park Road, they used a "tick book" instead of money.

His sister Hilda made the books, all people used them. They paid at the end of each week when they got their wages. He saw his pals playing Ralio, so joined in, and forgot about the milk, which was for teatime. He was running very fast with a boy chasing him down the entries. As he crossed the street to go down another entry, he tripped on the kerb and went flying into an entry, which had a telegraph pole in it. His head hit the pole and he was knocked out. The other boys thought he was dead, and went for help. he was out for about a quarter of an hour. He had a big lump on the side of His forehead. So he went home without the milk, which, they were all waiting for. His dad was very angry and went to hit him. His sister Hilda and David stopped him. The lump was like an egg and, he could see it sticking out. His mum treated it, and then he went to bed until morning.

As there was no electric just gas, Dad made a wireless. It was a big eleven-valve set. He could get most places in the world on it. Only he was allowed to touch it. It worked off batteries or an accumulator. They also had a medical coil, which also worked off the accumulator. It was a large coil set on a block of mahogany A long brass tube went into the centre of it, and there were wires coming from the coil and to a make- and- break which had a pair of contacts worked by a flat bronze spring. The coil's electrics pulled the contacts together and the spring parted them. There was an adjuster to set the spring, also wires going to two copper tubes which, you held in your hand one in your left and one in your right. (positive and negative). The electricity then went into your body. If you pulled the brass tube out more the current would get stronger. All the family had the electric treatment. His mum holding one copper tube and his dad holding the other copper tube. Then they all held hands to make a chain, one end holding his mum's other hand and one end holding his dad's other hand. It cured a lot of issues.

They used to play a game of "Tip it". One team was one side of the table. One team on the other side. They used a coat button. The team with the button, all hid their hands out of sight. The button was in someone's hand ready. All the team with the button put their hands closed on the table. Then one of the other team had to guess which hand the button was in. They had to say take that one off, touching that hand which was removed until they had guessed right. If it got to the last hand before they got it right, they had lost that game. So it started again, that was one game won by team A. If the team B guessed right then, they had won one game, and they then had the button. Each team member took turns in guessing which hand the button was in.

Norman's mum always had a cat. It used to catch birds in the park and mice from the stables near their house. It would bring the mice home and play with them. It used to let them go, then catch them again. After a while it would stop playing, and eat them, leaving the tail. His mum used to buy a full fish. She gave the head, tail and fins to the cat. He would growl and purr then, when finished, he would have a nap.

One day while Norman was playing in Hullard Park in Old Trafford; he was with some other boys, in some bushes which had railings round them to keep people out. The park keeper came and was very angry. Another boy and Norman ran out of the Park gates, but the park keeper had a bike and came after them. They split up the park keeper came after Norman. He pulled up near the pavement that Norman was on and as he was getting off, Norman went round the back of the bike and crossed the road. He was determined to catch Norman and Norman was determined he wouldn't, as he knew that if he did and his dad knew, he wouldn't half cop it. So he kept running all over Manchester. Norman thought he would never stop chasing him. Norman finally ran into a back yard of a derelict house. He ran down the steps into the cellar waiting to see if he was following him. He saw him put his bike against the wall and start to come down the steps, so Norman ran upstairs into the front bedroom. He could hear him coming up. There were no window panes in the bedroom, so he jumped right through the window, onto the garden below. It hurt his ankles, but he wasn't stopping for anything, the park keeper didn't jump, by the time he got out of the house Norman was gone. He cut through the churchyard onto City Road and onto Cornbrook Park Road where he lived. he waited, but the park keeper didn't appear.

When going up town to church and Sunday school, Norman and his sister Edna used to watch the children of the Bluecoat School going into Manchester Cathedral. They had black three corner hats on, blue frock coats, knee breeches, white stockings and black buckle shoes. The Bluecoat School is now Cheetham School of Music.

Not far from there was an area called Red Bank. There was a school called Red Bank Ragged School.

Norman was mad about football. They wouldn't let him play for the school team, as he had no football boots. When he went shopping with his mum on Saturday mornings, he used to stop at the shoe shop's window looking at the football boots. Cheap ones were four shillings and nine pence. The best ones called "Timpson's Knockouts", were seven shillings and ten pence. They had nice toes which were flat on the top. The cheap ones had a round toe top. He looked in that shop on Stretford Road every time they went passed it. But he could only dream. He had to wait a long time before he got a real football. When he did, he put dubbing on it, rubbed it into the stitches and leather, knowing it had to last a long time. Playing on the red shale in the park wore holes in it. So he took it to the cobbler who put patches on it. He kept taking it to him for patches until one day he said, "I can't put any more patches on this, Son, and there is no room for any more, you will have to get a new one." Norman thought he had better take it to a museum. So he had to wait till he was working to buy his own. He used to play football in his gym shoes they called them galoshes in those days.

Norman used to have to go to the coal yard for coal. They had big iron and wood trucks with iron wheels. Norman pulled the trucks home, tipped the coal down the coal grid and then took the truck back. He also went to the gasworks at Medlock Street for coke in an old pram. Norman's brother David taught him how to pull his bike to pieces and put it back properly, set things and mend punctures. Norman's brother David used to go out on his bike on a Sunday all day. He went a long way to Wales, Staffordshire, and Cheshire. Norman used to go camping on his bike for the weekend. He used to go on a Friday after work with his pals to Cheshire and come back on Sunday evening. They used to go swimming in the River Bollin, and cooking on the campfire; it was great.

One of the games they used to play was "Whip and Tops". You had to hit the tops with a stick that had string tied to it, called a whip. The boys had racing tops which, though they didn't spin as well as the girls' tops, would shoot along the road for racing. The girls' tops were big tops that would spin a long time and you didn't have to whip them as much. They would put chalk of different colours on top, so they made nice patterns while spinning. Girls did skipping solo, and sometimes with a long rope, with a girl at each end turning it. They would run and jump in it sometimes five or six at a time. The boys played "Ralio", which involved two teams and a den, they used a works doorway. When one of the team was caught, he was put in the den. A guard was watching over the den. The boys who were not caught had to try and get those of their team free from the den by touching the door of the den and shouting "Ralio" without getting caught. If they did those caught would all run out. The teams would take it in turn to be the one who was out. There were boundaries, which you had to keep within when you were out.

There was a large derelict house in Cornbrook Park Road. It had no windows or doors, so the children used to play in it. One day the boys found out there was a blank room upstairs. (A blank room is a room with no doors or windows in it.) So they knocked a big hole in the wall on one side and another hole on the other side. Inside there were no floorboards on the beams, so they had to be careful not to put their feet in between the beams and go through. They got used to it and walked on the beams from one hole to the other. After a while they could run on the beams, so had plenty of fun chasing each other. Then they got some thick corrugated paper and put it over all the beams like floorboards. They then had to be very careful to see where the beams were. After a while they could tell where they were as they got dirty with their walking on them. They had a lot of fun doing that. One day a big fat policeman was chasing them. They had been playing football in the street, after he had told them not to. They ran into the derelict house, up the stairs. He was after them and they went into the hole in the blank room and out at the hole on the other side. The policeman followed them, not knowing about the floorboards. He put both feet between the beams and through the ceiling below getting stuck. They saw two legs sticking through the ceiling and had a good laugh, and then off they went. They had to keep a sharp look out for him after that for a while.

Some days a man would come round with a barrel organ on wheels. The man would turn a handle to make the music; he could turn a dial to make different tunes. Sometimes there was a monkey on the barrel organ (collecting the money). The children danced and sang to the music. The street lamps were gaslights. A man had to light them. He had two poles, one with a hook to turn the gas on and another with a lit taper to light the gas mantel. The main road lights were very tall, so the men who lit them had longer poles.

The milkman had a pony and trap, with large urns of milk. People came out with jugs. He had measures to give you what you asked for, half a pint, or one pint or more. There were no milk bottles then.

It was very rare to see an aeroplane. It was also rare to see a black man. They would see one or two Chinese. There were plenty of policemen, sometimes in two s. They had whistles to signal to each other, also sticks to knock on the pavement at night to signal other policemen. That's how they caught criminals. They always had a watch, so you could ask them the time. Norman's dad told him to ask them, when he said he wanted Norman home at a certain time.

They used to make buggies out of prams. They had four wheels and a plank on the two axels; the front two were moveable for steering. They took them to a hill called Cookie Hill near the swimming baths at Northumberland Road.

Norman could go to town on the tram for a half penny, where it was one penny for adults. The lorries were steam powered and had fires like a train. There was a tray underneath to catch the hot cinders, some of which would fall on the road. They had single deck buses at first. Then they got double decker buses. These used to sway and lean over badly. People used to think they would fall over, so they didn't want to use them.

It was a long time before they got better suspension, then they were fine.

It was very rare there was a murder. When there was a special newspaper was printed and newspaper boys ran about the streets shouting "Special!". he saw many people "bandy" because of malnutrition. Some had knees which nearly touched the ground when walking. Others were worse, they had to have their legs broken and turned so the shin was curved towards the front. Norman used to notice very poor people who had large families, the boys in just a shirt and short trousers with no shoes or socks. The girls had a frock with no socks or shoes, and no coats during winter. He saw them running about in bare feet.

There was a song in Manchester about it called: -

In Barefoot Days.

In barefoot days, when we were just a couple of kids,
In barefoot days, oh boy the things we did.
We'd go down to a shady nook, with a bent pin for a hook,
We'd fish all day, and fish all night,
But the ruddy old fish refused to bite.
We'd slide and slide, down some old cellar door,
We'd slide and slide, till our pants got torn,
Then we'd have to go home, lie in our bed,
While the mother got busy with the needle and thread.
Oh boy! What joys, we had in barefoot days.

The churches used to feed the people with bread and soup. The hospitals were also poor. On Shrove Tuesday (Pancake Day), the students would go all over Manchester and outer lying districts collecting money for the hospitals. They went into shops, factories, schools and everywhere they could think of. They also had a big pageant down the main roads in Manchester, dressed like clowns. All the people lined the side of the roads. The students held blankets for people to throw money in. Then at night they tossed pancakes in the air, in the city centre squares. It was a great day for all.

At whit week people got dressed up in new clothes. There were two big processions, one on Monday for the Protestant church and the other one for the Catholics on Friday. Both were very long. They were classed as holidays.

One night Norman woke up and found his brother David was talking in his sleep. he couldn't tell what he was saying, so he started laughing. It woke George up making him cross and he said "What are you laughing about? You have woken me up!" he said "It's David, he's talking in his sleep. Listen." David started again, which started George and Norman laughing. That woke David up; he said "What are you two laughing about?" They couldn't tell him because they were laughing too much. That set David off laughing, which made them worse. They knew he didn't know what he was laughing about (laughing at himself). The girls woke up. Hilda and Edna wanted to know what They were laughing about. So Norman thought he would have some fun. He told Edna, that David was talking in his sleep. She said "What did he say?" he thought he would tell her something daft, Norman said," David had said, three bananas are worth a candle if you hit them on the head with a match." They roared laughing, so all five of them were at it. Their dad was doing his nut. "I`ll sort the lot of you out if I have to come up there! Get to sleep the lot of you!" Norman had to put his head under the pillow so that he couldn't hear him, because he couldn't stop laughing right away.

One day Norman's mum said to his dad, when he had been hitting him; "You are knocking the devil in him, not out!"

One day when Norman was eleven, he was on his way home from watching the ships at Trafford Bridge. He passed some garden houses. There was a path between each pair of semi-detached houses, which sloped down leading to the back. He went down one of those passages and stopped to watch a man putting a new back door on. The passage was on a slope towards the door. Norman was standing half way down so the garden was above him. Some children were playing there. They pushed a stone slab off the top of the wall on to Norman. It hit him with a glancing blow on his head and left shoulder. This knocked him over. Norman's head was cut and pouring with blood. He got up and ran to the children's house. The front door was open and he knocked on the door. A woman came and when she saw him she nearly fainted at him being covered in blood! Norman's white shirt was red. She put a cloth on his head to stop the bleeding and took him to a doctor. The doctor cut Norman's hair off near the wound and stitched it, then dressed it. He then went home on his own. On the way he was passing a works called Veno's, which made cough mixture, soon after 5.30pm when the women who worked there were all coming out. Whilst he was waiting to cross the road, two of them asked, "What has happened to you, Son, have you been run over?" he told them what happened. "Come on love we will take you across the road and home." So the two of them took him home, and when she saw Norman his mum nearly fainted as well.

Norman's brother George used to complain about crumbs in the bed, with him eating in bed, after he got no meals for punishment. They had night shirts to sleep in, so the crumbs scratched his bum. Norman used to get up in the middle of the night and go downstairs and find something to eat. He would make himself a butty. When on punishment he had to stay upstairs and he used to play on the stairs. There were five stairs, then a small landing, then thirteen stairs. At the bottom was the door to his Mum and Dad's bedroom. He first learnt to jump the five stairs on to the landing. The thirteen stairs were a lot harder to jump and it took him a while to find a way to do it. He would lean as far as he could, grip the banister with his right hand and, his left hand on the wall, and jump. Then as his body was passing his right hand, he let that hand slide down the banister and his left hand slide along the wall. His two feet would land on the mat outside his Mum and Dad's door. He used to do it during the day when no one was about. Early one Sunday morning, he was awake and everyone else was asleep. He got the pillow and gave George a whack on his face. He was hopping mad and he got out of bed, and went after him. He jumped the five stairs, then the thirteen stairs. Bang! he landed on the mat outside his Mum and Dad's bedroom door. His dad woke up and shouted, "What's going on?". George retreated quickly back into bed. Norman went into the living room and hid behind the settee and all went quiet. His dad didn't get up so he stayed in the living room. George couldn't jump the stairs, so he had no chance of catching Norman.

Norman's Dad went on holidays on his own on a motorbike and he found places, for Norman's Mum to take the children on a week's holiday. The places were mostly in Wales on farms. One place he remembered was Rhos-on —Sea; from there they would go to Conway, Colwyn Bay, and Llandudno. Norman never saw him take Mum out, or the children. He would go out on his own. He had a vile temper, if anyone went against him on matters, he would bring his fist down on the table and shout, "I'm the master in this house," Norman thought he was going to smash the table.

One day they were playing cricket in the street using the lamppost as wickets, when two plain clothes policemen came to catch them. One was at one end of the street and one was at the other, so they couldn't get away. They asked for their names and addresses. Norman wouldn't give them his so they asked the other boys what it was. One of them told them. Norman was holding the ball, which was his. They asked for it. he said, "You can't have it, it's my property." They said, "It's the court's property as evidence, until they decide to give it back to you. So Norman said, "If you want it you can get it." He threw it a long way down the street, but they didn't go for it, so it was lost. They went to see Norman's parents, so his sister Hilda came for him to go home, he went home and they told his Dad what he had done. They said he would have to go to Strangeways Juvenile Court. A letter would be sent regarding the time and date.

Norman's dad was very angry, but didn't hit him. When he went to court, his dad had to be with him and all the other boys were there with their parents. They were lined up before a magistrate and others. The magistrate gave them all a dressing down and warnings. Then he said, "You can all go, but Moors stay behind." He then gave Norman another telling off and a warning and then fined him ten shillings. His Dad was standing behind him, so he turned around and asked him for ten shillings. If looks could have killed he would have been dead. So the fine was paid and they went home. Norman said to his mates," The wind is in the east for now." (which means his dad is quiet for the time being.)

One time when Norman's Dad was hitting hin, he said to his dad, "Wait till I am 18. I'll give you a good hiding then." Then his dad really gave him a hiding, the family had to run out and get a policeman to stop him, or he would have killed him. The copper told him what for, and said, "If I have to come here again, I'll be taking you down to the station."

One time in the nineteen thirties Manchester United was in the second division, and almost in the third. Norman used to wait outside the ground for the gates to open at three quarter time, to let people out. All those outside went in and Norman was one of them. It was one shilling and six pence for first team matches and nine pence for second team matches. Football players before the war were on about £20 a week.

The ground outside was black cinders, pools of water, stones, bricks and other rubbish. While they were waiting to go in there was plenty of entertainment. A man tied up in a straitjacket would get out of it. Another man was tied up with rope and another man with chains. They would ask anyone to tie them up. They always got out (very clever). Another man would chew razor blades and swallow them. He would also stones and marbles. He would swallow a pocket watch, and hold on to the chain, then ask people to hear the watch ticking inside him. His mouth was full of blood when chewing the razor blades. They were lucky if they got 200 in to pay to watch, as people were very poor and out of work. There were no benefits then.

One day Norman's dad was after him; he forgot what for and he ran into the bathroom and bolted the door. His dad said, "Open this door Norman or I'll burst it open!" Norman opened the bathroom window (a sash cord one) and climbed onto the sill and then lowered himself down, until he was hanging on the sill by his fingers and he let go. The window was over the back doorsteps. There was a large flat step, which he landed on. He hurt his ankles and then climbed over the fence into St Georges Park. He stayed there for two or three hours until his dad cooled down and then he went home. His dad had bust the small bolt off the door and he got the shock of his life when he saw the bathroom empty.

One day when Norman was thirteen, he was having a lift home on a lad's bike. Norman was sitting on the crossbar of his friend's bike and as they pulled into the kerb, near home, another lad on a bike came alongside them and pushed them over. Norman fell with his right arm under him as he hit the curb, and broke his arm. He went home into the living room and sat on the settee holding his arm. Norman's Mum came in and she said, "What are you holding your arm like that for?" She then looked and saw it was broken and she said, "Ah, your dad will have to see that." And Norman said "I don't want him to see it." When his dad saw it he said, "Take him to the doctor." The doctor looked at it and said, "Take him to the Manchester Royal Infirmary." They looked at it then painted his arm from hand to elbow with iodine. They put his arm in a sling and said, "Bring him back in the morning, and we will set it with splints." Norman went next day and it took three people to set it, one doctor and two nurses. The splints were made of metal and padding. They bound his arm up tight with bandages, put a sling on and said to come back in six weeks' time.

Norman's brother George wanted to learn public speaking. He was eighteen and took Norman with him to Platt Fields one Sunday afternoon and there were a lot of groups of men. A man was standing on a box talking with people asking him questions. Norman didn't know what it was all about, but thought he must be clever to answer all the questions. There were political and religious groups.

CHAPTER 2

Starting Work

Norman left school at fourteen, he wanted to be a plumber because he saw men coming in the house mending lead pipes, when they had burst, he didn't know what he wanted really. His Dad never gave him any guidance. There were no jobs for apprentice plumbers at the employment office, so they sent Norman to W.H. Whitham & Co near where he lived as an apprentice fitter engineer. The company made steel rules with gauges and degrees for machines and some were curved. The markings and numbers were burnt in with acids. The rules were with an acid proof varnish, then the markings and numbers were put on by a machine. Then they were put in a trough, which was lead lined with pitch over it to prevent the acid burning into the lead. Two types of acid were used. The trough had to be rocked slowly, so the acid would flow over the rules and let the air get to it. Then it had to be rocked again until the markings were burnt in deep enough. One of Norman's jobs was rocking the trough. When deep enough the rules were taken out and washed then with paraffin removing the varnish. They were then polished with emery cloth to finish the job. Norman worked there for ten months and he wanted to leave and get a better job, so he could learn more. Norman asked his Mum if he could have Saturday morning off to go and look for a job. The week was a 46 hour including Saturday morning. Norman's wages were ten shillings a week. His Mum said, "What do you want to leave there for? You are near home and can come home for dinner". he said, "I am not learning enough. "She said "Ok.". So he got up early and went looking around Trafford Park Industrial area asking for any vacancies. Norman went all over the place with no luck. It was getting near dinnertime and he went out of Trafford Park, cut across to Warwick Road Railway Station (electric line), and on to Elsmore Road. Norman started asking engineering firms as he went along Herbert Hunts was the first one. Norman's sister Dora was a skilled turner there one time. Norman got to E., Boydell's. It was 11.45am. They closed at noon so he didn't think he had much chance, but in he went. To his delight he got a job as an apprentice fitter. He had to give a weeks' notice at Whitham's. Then he started on the Monday week at E Boydell's. The wages were better, eleven shillings and ten pence. The firm made contractors plant, dumpers and loading shovels. There were about ten apprentices some on fitting, some in the machine shop.

When Norman was fifteen, he was smaller than some of the lads of his age. One day he was having an argument with three other lads, Ken Brockelhurst, Ken Gill, and Charlie Daniels, who was the biggest. A fight started between Ken Brockelhurst and Norman. Norman made his nose and mouth bleed so he gave in. The other two didn't like it; they were on his side, so they started saying nasty things to Norman. Suddenly Charlie Daniels hit Norman with his fists, (on the sly) in his left eye. As Norman put his hand to his eye, he hit Norman in the other eye, so he was at a disadvantage. Norman fought back and gave him a few good punches. Then a man who was passing on the other side of the road ran over and stopped the fight. He said, "I can see what is going on here. Its three on to one, you are all bigger than him, you cowards!" Then he said to Charlie Daniels, "You are as big as me. Now hit me," When nothing happened, the man said, "No you can only hit someone smaller than yourself, you bully!" "Get off home you," he said to Norman. He didn't want to go so he made him go. When Norman got home, he went to the bathroom, filled the wash basin with cold water, and put his face in it. His Mum came in to the bathroom and saw his face. "Have you been fighting again?" She said. She told Norman off then left him to it. She was almost as hard as his Dad.

It was a code of honour, when fighting, that you didn't hit on the sly, had to wait till your opponent was ready, no hitting when down.

There was no kicking, biting scratching. (Fists only.) You were a coward if you did.

While Norman was at Boydell's, he was working on a long bench with vices on, with some other lads, making parts for the dumpers. he had to start getting a tool kit together. Some he bought, some he made himself. The men fitters showed him how and gave him things. Norman made his Mum a shopping trolley out of old trolley wheels and axle. Then he went to Blind Workshop and bought a large d-shaped basket. he bolted that to the frame. She needed it, as she didn't have Norman to help her now he was working. When it got near Christmas, the year he was 15, the firm had a dance party at the Old Trafford Technical Institute on the Stretford Road corner of Northumberland Road. The bandleader was Victor Sylvester who became famous and appeared on television in later years. Norman's dad said, "Seeing as though you are going to a dance party, I want you home by 10.30pm." Norman was having a good time with his new workmates and then he looked at the clock on the wall. It was 10.45pm. He knew then how Cinderella felt, so he ran all the way home. It was 11:00pm. when he got there.

The house was in darkness and everyone was in bed. Norman was standing on the second step, which was a large one. The wall of next door's works where they kept their packing cases was at the back of him. Norman knocked on the doorknocker and listened at the letterbox to see who was coming. It was the boss. He started to unbolt the bolts and chains, then the lock. He opened the door and gave Norman a mighty punch, which sent him flying against the wall. He wasn't knocked out, but said to himself, "I'm not waiting for any more of that!" he got up and ran through the gate and down towards City Road, he also said to himself, "I'm staying out all night." Norman's dad went into the house and got Norman's two brothers up, George and David. He told them to find him and bring him home. David was 25. George was 20. It was a cold night. Norman was at the top of Cornbrook Park Road, wondering where he could go. His dad was shouting Norman's name, waking the entire neighbourhood up. Norman could see his brothers looking for him. Norman's dad had to shut up shouting as people told him to pipe down, and it was cold. Norman dodged them all and went home, leaving them looking for him. His Mum said, "They are out looking for you." he said," I know they are." She said, "You'd better get to bed." So he did. They gave up after a while and also went to bed. Norman was asleep when George got in bed and he was careful not to wake him. Next morning all was quiet and nothing was said about it. 'Mum must have told his dad to keep the peace. After that Norman wanted to leave home. He saw an advert in the Manchester Evening News. "Boys wanted 15 to 18. sheep farming in Australia". Norman asked his Mum, who said, "You will have to ask your Dad about that." he said, "I'm not asking him, please ask him for me." She said she would. Norman kept asking until they both said he could go. Norman was all set to go and was at Rigby's Shipping Agents in Manchester. The papers had to be signed by both his parents. Norman had five pounds to last him until he got fixed up with a sheep farm. It was going to take six weeks on a ship to get there and a lot of lads were going. Norman's parent's changed their minds and wouldn't sign the papers, so Norman went home very disappointed.

In the second week in January 1938 Norman didn't go to work one morning he went up to town to join the Royal Navy. Norman passed as boy signaller. He would have been in for fifteen years as it was three year's plus twelve year's. The first three years was classed as boy's service and didn't count. The man gave him some papers to take home. He said, "Get your parents to sign these and then bring them back," Norman's dad looked at them and tore them up, so he had to wait to get away.

Norman was doing well at Boydell's so when he was sixteen and a half, Norman and two other apprentices were put on building a 2 yard dumper with a new man each to show them how. The other two and Norman had been working with different fitters at different stages of building the dumpers. They had never done one from start to finish. The man he got to show was thirty five years old. he wasn't sure himself.

Norman had to show him and tell him what to do. He smoked Capstan Full Strength. He didn't like the smell of them, so Norman used to go for a walk until he had finished. Some of the time, when he went off, he was stuck and didn't know what to do. He was lost. Norman was stuck himself sometimes and had to ask the fitters he had worked with. They managed to get it done. The test driver put the petrol in and drove it out to be tested. It passed. Was he glad, that was over!

One day Norman was working in the fitting bay at Boydell's on a long bench at the vice. In front of him was the wall of the machine shop. The machine shop area, used to be Oldfield's Bakery, which, had closed down. Before it closed Boydell's needed more space, and so, took the building over.

They took the big windows out leaving large holes in the wall. One day he could see a lad called Fisher working a capstan lathe. Fisher was a bit older than Norman was and very cocky he was too.

He started to say things to annoy Norman. One word led to another and Fisher said he would see Norman outside after work. he said, "Ok, see you then." Others heard what was going on and so a crowd gathered there to see the fight. A man who was a pattern maker was to be the referee. They went at it hammer and tong. Norman slipped and fell down. Fisher stood over Norman. He saw blood dropping from Fishers face. Norman said, "Stand back while I get up." He wouldn't do that. The ref made him. So Norman went at him again. After a short while, Fisher said, "ok you win, I've had enough." They shook hands and went home. Everyone had been shouting for Ike, which was Norman's nickname.

When the war started, the men at Boydell's were told that Direction of Labour was coming in soon. When it did, they would have to stay for the duration of the war and would not be able to leave.

So if anyone wanted to leave they would have to do so now and some did leave. Then Boydell's also asked the apprentices. Three left Norman was one of them and he was seventeen. Norman's next job was at Hills Aircraft on Trafford Park, on shifts 6am to 2pm. It was the first day, it was foggy and as Norman was on his bike passing Glovers Cables, where there were railway lines and tramlines. He was riding between the tramlines and a tram was coming behind him ringing its bell and he had to get out of the way and in doing so Norman finished up on the railway lines and fell off his bike. Norman's front wheel was all bent, so he had to carry it to work, arriving late.

They put Norman to work in a sawmill. he said, "I am an apprentice fitter engineer and this is not my job," so they said they had nothing for him there.

Norman left on the first day and the next job was Donald Browns on Moss Lane. Hulme District.

They were making alloy fittings for aircraft. Norman did the threads after the parts were machined for about two months and then he asked the foreman for something better to do. He put Norman on drilling machines, which he did for a week. Then Norman asked the foreman again, Norman told him, he was doing those things at fourteen and was now nearly eighteen and the foreman told Norman he had nothing else for him and he had better leave. Norman said," Yes I better had." So Norman left and the next Job he had was at a musical instrument makers in Jackson Street, Hulme District.

Picture (Taken on H M S RODNEY in Scapa Flow, Norman age 19)

CHAPTER 3

The War Started

The war started in September in 1939, and Norman went to join the Royal Navy on 4th December 1940 on his 18th Birthday.

When the bombing started the Manchester Blitz. It was a Saturday night and, Norman was out with the two Morgan brothers (James and Donald), who lived next door but one. The guns were firing so shrapnel was falling, some big pieces and hot too. They had to go in a shelter at East Union Street police station. After an hour or more, they noticed the bombs were coming in waves, with an interval of about fifteen minutes between waves. Norman and his friend's decided to run home when the next lull came. They ran as fast as they could and as they entered Cornbrook Park Road, a few lads they knew told Norman his house was on fire. they were at the top of the road near City Road where as they lived at the bottom end. They ran down to it and a fire engine was there. The fire was under control and the top of the house, including my bedroom was burnt out. Norman went to go in and a fireman asked, "Where are you going?". Norman said, "I live here. ". He said, "You can't go in there. Your family is in the shelter down the road. ". Norman found his family and stayed there till morning. The house had been hit by three incendiary bombs, which caused it to burn very quickly. It was a good job Norman's two brothers and him were not in it. Norman lost everything he had, but for the clothes he had on him. In the morning he went to look at all the damage. There was a timber yard near where he lived. It had large trees on the ground waiting to be cut into planks. The doors were open and inside was a big land mine stuck between two trees. It had a green parachute attached to it. When these landmines were first being dropped, there were men putting sand on the incendiary bombs as they fell to the ground. The Germans used them first to light up the targets at night. When they saw the landmine coming down by parachute, they thought it was a pilot bailing out so they ran to get him. As they got near they saw it was a bomb. They shouted, "It's a bomb." and about turned and ran for their lives.

The one in the timber yard had not gone off, because it was delayed action, and they had to lie down before the mechanism inside started working. A naval bomb expert came to look at it with the police. He told them to evacuate the area, so the police made all the people get out of their homes and they cleared the area. They made the bomb dead. Norman went to the rest centre at the old Stretford Town Hall with one of the Morgan lads, Donald. Norman didn't know where the rest of the family had gone. While Norman was in the rest centre he slept in a bunk there that Sunday during the day, he was tired having had no sleep on Saturday night with the bombing and Norman also got his meals there. Norman's brother David came home on leave as he was in the army, David got called up with the first lot of conscripts. David was looking for the family and he came to the rest centre and found Norman. He wanted to know where the rest of the family was and Norman told David, he didn't know. It was getting late on Sunday afternoon and all was quiet. David said, "Let's go and find the family. ". So, they set of down Chester Road, then Talbot Road; and the bombing started again. They went into people's gardens and lying down on the soil near garden walls and hedges to shelter from the bombs. They were after Trafford Park industrial area, which was not far away. They managed to reach Trafford Bar, which was the end of Talbot Road. There was a shelter there so they spent the night in it. No one else was in it except the three of them. They went to sleep on the bunks there with no blankets. It was cold and damp so they didn't get much sleep. In the morning they went into a garage nearby which, had been made into a fire station.

The firemen gave them a mug of tea and a sandwich. They must have looked a mess after lying in the soil in the gardens, and tired and hungry. Then they went near home asking where the family was. People told them to try the Zion Church on Stretford Road near Jackson Street. They went there and found them all. The family were pleased to see David and Norman as they had been worried about them.

It was Monday the 24th December 1940. Norman went to the post office to get the mail and there was a letter from the Royal Navy. Norman's calling up papers it said Norman would have to go to Keyham, Devonport near Plymouth, HMS Drake Barracks. There was a railway ticket for him to Plymouth from Manchester and Norman had to be there on January 3rd 1941.

CHAPTER 4

Off To War

January 2nd 1941. Norman went to London Road station (now called Piccadilly) to catch the midnight train to Plymouth North Road Station. Norman's Dad went with him to the tram stop to see him off. He shook his hand and said goodbye. There was no hug or any sign of love. Norman felt hurt, unwanted. Here he was going off to war he may never see him again. Norman thought,' what a family I've got!' Norman arrived at the station where there were plenty of people waiting for the train. Some were young men with girlfriends, saying their goodbyes. The train was packed and he managed to get a seat but a lot had to stand up. Norman had no money, just a few sandwiches his Mum had managed to put up for him, with the clothes he stood up in and nothing else. He tried to get some sleep as the train moved off. The bombing was going on in a lot of places as they went on their way. The train stopped in a tunnel twice to miss the bombs.

They arrived at Plymouth at 3pm, so the journey had taken fifteen hours. At the station were two lorries with canvas tops and RN painted on the side. The Chief Petty Officers, he had noticed they had long gaiters on their legs. The soldiers had short ones. The gaiters came almost up to their knees. They asked for all who were for HMS Drake to line up whilst they checked their papers then they told them to get into the lorries. Off they went to Drake barracks. It was a few miles to a place called Keyham in Devonport. They arrived about 4pm and they were taken to the new entrants' mess. It was the last block near the parade ground. The first job was to give them a hammock and show them how to make it and sling it. They taught them how to lash it up and stow it in the morning. When lashing it, it had to have seven turns (like the seven seas). There was a straw mattress with covers and one blanket. When that was sorted out it was time for supper at 6pm and they were marched to a large dining hall. They sat ten at each table, five each side. They had a good dinner. Norman told the Chief who was in charge of us that he had been bombed out, he had only what he stood up in. He fixed Norman up with a towel, soap and comb. he hadn't started shaving so was ok for that. They had nothing to do then till next day. Norman went for a walk to look around the barracks and he found there was a cinema, and asked if he could go in and he told them he was a new entrant who had just arrived today. They said it was ok. It was cold outside so he was glad to get in. There were two pictures on. One small one a comic, and the big one was a Western. When Norman came out it was dark and cold so he was eager to get to the mess, then all of a sudden, someone jumped on his back. Norman swung around shaking him off and hit out with his fist. Norman landed a four penny one right in his face. It was a sailor. He didn't, wait for any more and ran off into the dark. Norman thought `This is a right place I've come to!' Norman got back to the mess and put his hammock up. he found it difficult to get into it, and not so comfortable. he was tired and he soon was off to sleep, after they had blown a bugle and said, "Pipe down," and blown a whistle on the loudspeaker. Norman was woken up by the same loudspeaker and, bugle blowing reveille at 6.30 am. Norman got up and got washed and dressed. The chief came in and told them that they would be going for a medical after breakfast. There were twenty of them going for a medical. They went into a large room and were told to line up before a doctor, who examined them. After that they were shown around the barracks for the rest of the day and they were told they were having their trade test tomorrow, in the dockyard.

The next day, after breakfast, they were marched to the dockyard for their trade test. A chief artificer was then in charge of them.

He gave them each a forged steel block, 2 5/16" by 2 5/16", a square, two 12" flat files, one smooth, one rough, one hammer, one flat chisel, one centre punch. They had the use of a surface plate with blue marking. They had one scribing block, a 6" rule. The officer told them that they had to make the block into a 2" by 2" square. It had to be flat on all sides, smooth, square, and they had twelve hours to do it in.

The chisel was soft, the files worn and they were not allowed to use the grindstone to sharpen the chisel or use any machines in the workshop. They could only use the tools given. The steel block, being forged had a hard skin on it. The files were not much use. Norman was the only one who was eighteen. All the others were older. Some were in their 20's and some were in their 30's. When they saw the tools to do the job, they complained, but to no avail. They were all volunteers, They could walk out and go home and some did. They must have had money to get home or hitch hiked. They only had a one-way ticket and out of fifteen, seven went home. Norman had no money to get home, and didn't fancy going home anyway. He had joined the navy to get away from home. So, he got stuck into the job. It was very hard indeed and it took him fourteen hours.

When Norman went to see the Rear Admiral Engineer with his job, he watched him test it in a gauge with feelers. He then turned to Norman, and said in a deep voice, "You have taken fourteen hours," Norman's heart sank and he was thinking of going home, where he didn't want to go, "but you have made a good job of this son. I am going to recommend you for engines in the Fleet Air Arm."

Norman was so relived and excited to get what he wanted.

After that he was sworn in and signed the papers accepting the king's shilling. Now Norman had for his kit fore & aft rig, he was to wear it before breakfast the next morning. You were not allowed in the dining hall unless you were properly dressed. Norman was up early to get dressed and the collars were stiff ones rounded at the corners. The tie was black and every time he tried to fasten his front stud the tie kept slipping out and, try as he may, he couldn't do it. So he got no breakfast in the morning as he had to be properly dressed for drill that morning. Norman's collar was in a right mess, when he fell in with the squad. The petty officer said, "What have you been doing with your collar Moors?" Norman told him he had never worn one of these collars before. He said, "Get someone to show you tomorrow, and put a clean collar on. ". We had six collars in our kit. We had to wear them until we had finished our discipline training. Then we could wear semi-stiff collars, pointed at the corners, not rounded. he also had trouble with the underwear, which was flannel vests with long sleeves, boxer shorts, also flannel and they made Norman itch all over, so he couldn't wear them. he thought, 'I'll give them to my Dad, He wore flannel.' So, as soon as Norman got some pay, he went to the pursers store and he bought six pointed semi-stiff collars and three singlet's, three underpants (boxer type), made of winceyette. Norman's pay was three shillings and ten pence per day. he made an allowance to his mother of ten shillings per week, which left him sixteen shillings and ten pence per week. Out of that was his kit upkeep allowance. They did a week of drilling on the parade ground. All their kit had to have their name on it as did kit bag and hammock and blankets. Some things they used to paint on or use marking ink, some things, you could sew your name on. They had to have a swimming test and they went to the swimming baths in the barracks. The instructor said, "It is not compulsory for you to be able to swim but I advise you to learn now, those who can swim on the right and those who can't on the left." The ones who could swim started their test and finished it. The ones who couldn't were told to jump in at the deep end. If they wouldn't they were thrown in. Norman was so glad he could swim. The instructors had long bamboo poles, so anyone in difficulties had to hold on to the pole and be pulled to the side. They soon learned. Some took a week and some took longer. They then moved to Trevol Rifle Range in Torpoint, Cornwall. They went to learn about rifles and how to shoot them and they lived in wooden huts and there were twenty in the squad. They had to do guard duty at night for two hours each and they had four beats to guard, plus the main gate, checking people coming in. The sailors had a rifle and bayonet and five rounds of ammunition, and they were told not to have one in the spout (loaded). One night they were told some paratroopers had been dropped not far away, so they had to be on their guard and they also had a large torch. The officer used to come round to see if they were keeping watch, to make sure they weren't sleeping. The beat Norman was on one night was a path with trees and bushes on each side. It was dark and windy so there was a lot of rustling. Norman thought, 'Blow this! I am having this gun loaded.' thinking of paratroopers.

The officer came round. he shone the torch in Norman's face and shouted him to halt, "advance and be recognised." He didn't know Norman's gun was loaded. The officer came towards him and he saw who Norman was. He said, "Well done, Moors. I see you are on your toes, carry on." then he went away. Some 18 year old sailors went home. When they went out at night to go into Plymouth they had to go across the river on a ferry (Torpoint ferry). Plymouth was full of Polish servicemen, and French. The main street (Union Street) was a trouble spot, there was a place called the Snake Pit, which was full of girls and servicemen. Fights used to start, so the naval patrol had to go in and sort it out. The naval patrol had to walk up and down Union Street to keep things quiet. There was a place called Aggie Westerns where you could get a bed for the night for a shilling, and something to eat at a reasonable price and it was nice and clean. That was the first thing you did when you had night shore leave, book a bed before it was full up. You had to be twenty years of age before you could get night shore leave. On their way back to camp they used to buy a Hogie (Cornish pasty). They were very good and only tuppence hapenny each. A man used to stand near the dockyard gates shouting "oggie! Hot oggie!" If they didn't have enough money to go in a pub (beer was one shilling a pint) they went into scrumpy houses. These were like a pub but only sold cider at four pence a pint. They were only there two or three weeks. Then they were sent to a transit camp waiting to go on a course. The camp was Warner's Holiday Camp, in Puckpool near Ryde, Isle of Wight. The navy had taken the camp over. They were there six weeks and they were in the chalets. During their stay, Portsmouth and Southampton were being bombed and when the planes were returning they were on them before they could get to the shelters, and they had to lie on the floor under the beds. The planes had no bombs left so they machine-gunned their camp.

CHAPTER 5

Training Course

The sailors were at last on their way to go on the course. They took a train journey to Cannock Staffordshire and from there to a large RAF training camp in Rugeley. They arrived at 7pm, about a hundred of them. They were lined up in three ranks. A flight sergeant came out of the guard hut and put his arm between the front rank, then shouted three paces to the right march. That separated about 24 from the rest. "You will be on engines. The rest of you will be on airframes." Three others and Norman had been recommended for engines, so they told the flight sergeant. They were in the airframe bunch and they wanted engines not airframes. Also they were in the navy not the air force. He said, "I don't care what you have got. There is a war on, we have plenty of engine fitters, but are very short of airframe fitters. No matter who you are, you will have to do the airframe course. ". So, the next day he had to start the airframe course. They were billeted in nissen huts with bunk beds, using their hammock bedding.

The first subject was "Theory of Flight; how a plane takes off using flaps, ailerons, rudder controls, plus details of the aerofoil shape of the wings and propellers. They learned how to do it and an exam on the fifth day. "Second" control wires making and splicing making eyes - some open, some with a thimble on them and marriage splice. As the wire was extra flexible steel wire rope, it had seven strands and wire hearts, not like ships wire hawsers, which has six strands and hemp hearts. They had five days to learn it and an exam on the fifth day. "Hydraulics" was the third subject, on under carriage and suspension. They had five days to learn it and an exam on the fifth day. Fourth subject was sheet metal work, They learned how to rivet two pieces of aluminium together by hand. The rivet's heads must be in line, if not the rivet is weak. They also repairred damage on Sunderland Flying Boat. They had five days to learn it and an exam on the fifth day. The fifth subject was "Dope and Fabric". They had to sew a complete wing with new fabric, then pull tight and stitch at the trailing edge and dope it to shrink, tight as a drum. They had five days to learn it and an exam on the fifth day. Carpentry five days and Aero-carpentry five days. Make all joints on structure of wooden aircraft — five days. Fit panels to wings and fuselage and repair where damaged — five days.

On all subjects they had to do written theory as well as practical. Norman failed on carpentry and aero carpentry, he passed on all the ones before it. He was taken off the course and sent to the Fleet Air Arm Barracks in Lee on Solent. He went to HMS DAEDALUS after travelling down to the Fleet Air Arm Barracks.

The next day he had to see, the training commander. He offered Norman a lower position as air mechanic, Norman said, "What, on engines?" "No on airframes.", he replied. Norman said, "What's the use of that, I've just failed on airframes." "I'll go as a stoker. ". He said, "I don't think you should do that, you have not been in the navy five minutes. You don't know anything about the navy yet. Go as a seaman, you will then find out what you like and can do. You can always change then." So he was transferred back to HMS DRAKE to start as a seaman. Norman's service number was changed and he then started to be an ordinary seaman (OD). he was sent to HMS RALEIGH to be trained as a seaman, which was not far away. At the end of his training, the class he was in was asked for volunteers for minesweeping. They wanted six; they got more than six, so names had to be put in a hat and six drawn out, he was one of the volunteers, but his name didn't come out. So it-was back to HMS DRAKE to be drafted somewhere. That was to the Battleship Rodney in the wartime Fleet Anchorage in Scapa Flow, in the Orkney Islands. They got on a train in the barracks station. HMS DRAKE was locked in. It was 11pm; off they went to London and got there at about 4am.

They were given a packed lunch and then at 6am on a train to Scotland locked in again. They didn't get off 'till Perth, had a meal, then on the train again to Thurso at the top of Scotland. It was early morning when they got there. They had a nice cooked breakfast. Then they were on ship to take them to Scapa Flow. It was 2pm when it moved out. There was a hold at the stern, full of sailors. Some were soldiers and airmen going for defence of the islands. Norman looked down the hold. It was full of smoke, so he thought, `I'm not going down there,' he thought he might be seasick, as he had never been on a ship before. It was also Christmas Eve 1941. There was a well deck going from the bridge area to the forecastle, a short bow area. The well deck was about eight foot deep. It had a few vents sticking up and a large one for the engine room. So he sat on one of these vents. Some soldiers and airmen were standing with their backs to the forecastle in the well deck. When the ship went out, the bows went down and a great wall of seawater came towards them. The soldiers and airmen were in a waterfall and got knocked over. It also came towards Norman, it was up to his knees. There was a rail along the engine room vent, so he hung on to that, as the ship was starting to roll as well as pitch. One minute he was looking at the sea, big green waves, the next minute he was looking at the sky. he thought, "I can swim, but wouldn't like to swim in that. I'd better get out of here or I'll get washed overboard." he looked at the side near the bridge; saw the ladder to get out of the well deck. he thought. "I'll have to wait until it levels up, in between each roll. Then, run for the ladder before it goes over again." he did that, got to the ladder and couldn't go up until the ship levelled again. Then up the ladder as fast as he could, he stayed there. As there was a passage with a rail to hold on to so, he moved along that a bit away from the well deck, he stayed there until the ship got in. The sea there was the Pentland Firth. The North Sea and the Atlantic currents meeting and that's what makes it rough. They pulled alongside the Dunlose Castle, the depot ship in Scapa Flow. There were a lot of ships in the very big harbour. There were also a lot of small ones, called drifters. These took people to the ships they had to go to a C.P.O was shouting the names of ships, so those who were going onto the ones he shouted had to get onto that particular drifter. When he shouted Rodney, Norman and a lot more got on that one with their kit bag and hammocks. As they went across the harbour, it was cold and windy, with spray coming on them. Their kit bags and hammocks were getting wet. When they got on board they were given numbers of the mess they would be living in and taken to that mess. It was then 7pm and they had missed the last meal of the day, which was 6pm. They were given a plate and taken to the galley to get something to eat. It was Irish stew with a round of bread. Norman found his way back to the mess (number twenty two) on the port side, quarterdeck division, Norman had his meal, then the leading seaman, a Scouser who was in charge, introduced Norman to the rest of the mess.

The harbour Scapa Flow was made up of a number of islands with nets from one island to another to keep the U-Boats out. This was a weakness on one occasion, as a ship was coming in and the boom was open for it. A U-Boat came in to the harbour.

It torpedoed HMS Royal Oak and left again before the boom was closed. The Royal Oak was set on fire and blew up and sank, with very few survivors. Also during the 1914-1918 war the German Navy scuttled a number of their war ships in the harbour. That night he had to wait while those sailors who were already established on the ship and who had their regular billets (place to sling their hammocks), had put their hammocks up. There wasn't much room, so he had to sling his in the passageway, he turned in and was soon off to sleep. Norman was awakened shortly after midnight and sailor said, "You're in my billet", so Norman had to get out and find somewhere else to put up his hammock. The sailor had been on watch till midnight. What a Christmas!

Picture taken on leave, age 18. Pal Donald Morgan lived next door but two.

Walrus Sea Plane being lifted out of Scapa Flow

H.M.S. Rodney Scapa Flow

Troopship in Convoy Going to Africa
Via Indian Ocean

The leading seaman in charge of the mess was also captain of the Heads (toilets). Norman was moved after a couple of weeks to another mess on the other side of the ship, mess thirty one on the starboard side, where there was more room, and he could sling his hammock in the mess. In the passage way there was a notice board where daily orders for the next day were put up. You had to read them each evening, as they might concern you. Norman was then in "Top Division". They had aluminium lockers to keep their kit in, hammocks had to be stowed in a hammock space end up so your name which was painted on it could be seen. Reveille was at 6.30am (or 5 bells). A petty officer came around to check everyone got out of their hammocks right away. So it was, lash up and stow their hammock, then get washed and dressed, have breakfast, fall in at 8am on upper deck. They received details for jobs to be done. Some had special jobs, so didn't need to fall in.

Time By Bell
One bell every half hour 1 to 8 making 4 hours. 4,8,12noon, 4,8,12midnight
Watches

12 noon to 4pm was the Afternoon Watch. 4pm to 6pm was First Dog Watch. 6pm to 8pm was Second Dog Watch. 8pm to 12midnight was First Watch. 12am midnight to 4am was Middle Watch. 4am to 8am was Morning Watch, and 8am to 12pm was Forenoon Watch. The ship was divided into three watches. Cruising Stations had one watch on two watches off. Defence Stations, two watches on, one watch off. Action Stations had every watch on.

For Norman's Cruising Station, he was on the Bridge Communications, sometimes phones, and sometimes voice pipes. Other times he was on lookout. There were four lookouts, two on each side of the bridge. Norman's Action and Defence Station was in the starboard wing; 16" Magazine of B `Turret. There were four magazines to each gun turret, one starboard, one port, one after and one forward. There were six men in each mag. When they went in the mag they were locked in. There was a hatch, which was water tight as well as flash tight. There was no other way out. A loudspeaker was in every compartment of the ship, including the mags.

Another lookout position was above the bridge, called Air Defence Position. An officer had a microphone in that position, so he could speak to all the close range weapons, and tell which sector to open fire. The ship was divided into sectors, starting from the bows on each side, starboard and port. They were numbered 1-12 or more, green for starboard, red for port. Each sector overlapped each other by five degrees, so no plane could get through without being fired at. Guns could only open fire when their sector was told to open fire by the air defence officer. That saved ammunition. The directors that were above the bridge controlled the 16' and 6'guns. They also fired the guns from that position when they were ready to fire. When firing the 16" guns, the upper deck had to be cleared. They only fired a broadside twice whilst he was aboard. A broadride is, firing nine guns all at the same time. It did a lot of damage to the ship. After that they fired three gun Salvos; left guns of each turret, then centre guns of each turret, then right guns of each turret. 6" guns weren't a problem.

It took six packs of cordite each weighing 82 1 /2 lb. to fire one 16" shell. The cordite was in silk containers; two of them had gunpowder bags at one end. When loading the gun the third pack Had to have the red end facing the breech end, and the sixth pack the last one, had to have the red end near the breech. The reason being, gunpowder ignites better than cordite. Cordite gives off more powerful gases. In the magazine the cordite packs were in aluminium containers, three in each so one had a red end to it. Everything in a mag had to be non-spark material. Silk was used because it leaves no residue.

One time at Cruising Stations on the Middle Watch (12-4am) they used to sleep, as four hours is a long time to be doing nothing. If anything happened a bell rang and a pointer pointed to "load" or "secure" etc. This night Norman got left in the mag when all went out at 4am. So he couldn't get out till morning after 8am. Norman woke up found it was dark and thought the lights had fused. Then he couldn't hear anything. Norman shouted, no answer, so he crawled about and found no one in. It was a good job they didn't get torpedoed. Norman didn't get out till the sailors came to work in the cordite handling room on the other side of the mag. Norman heard their voices, so rang the bell. They got the key and let him out.

Norman had no breakfast, but didn't have to fall in as he had a special job as petty officers mess man. They were ordered not to open more than two containers of cordite at a time, as the fumes from the cordite gave them a bad headache.

Norman's first trip to sea on the Rodney was to Iceland. They were given arctic clothing, long johns of wool, sea boot stockings, white long and woollen, gloves, balaclavas and leather sea boots. It was January 1942 and they put into Reykjavik needing some supplies, which they got off a USA supply ship called SS Yukon. This was near them in the harbour. The yanks liked their jackknifes, which were bigger and stronger than their small ones. They gave them two cartons of Luck Strike cigarettes. 200 cigs in each carton for one of their jackknifes. They went on their mess deck, they had ice cream, and coca cola machines. Norman exchanged two jackknives for a pair of black, officer's shoes. They were the best shoes he had ever had, then and since. To Norman they were like gold. The American's gave them ice cream and told Norman, he could keep the spoon as a souvenir. Norman still has it with US stamped on it. After a few months of being around the Iceland area they went to Liverpool for a refit. They got three weeks leave, one watch starboard or port, first, then when the others came back, the other watch went on leave. It was not very nice being in dock, dirty and noisy, Norman was glad to get out again. A lot more ratings joined the ship at Liverpool. Their next trip was to Scapa and doing trials, testing new type 16" shells called direct impact. Other shells they had called armour piercing kept going right through a ship without going off. When testing the direct impact shells, they went off when they hit the sea, so they were very careful how they handled them, when loading them on to the ship. The shell rooms and shell handling room were on the deck above the magazines and the cordite handling room. When the 16" gun turrets on the top deck moved, everything below it moved in the centre of the compartments, shell handling room, cordite handling room, cordite hoist and shell hoist. That was about 1000 tons moved by hydraulics, right down to the bottom of the ship.

In 1925 the HMS Rodney was built by Cammell Lairds of Birkenhead. It was completed in August 1927. weighing 35.000 tons, 40,000 tons or more fully loaded. She had nine 16" guns; each of which could send a ton shell 22 miles. Her secondary armaments included twelve 6" guns — three twin gun turrets each side towards the stem. She was also the first ship to have radar. She also had torpedo tubes in the bows — 24", two 4'7" guns (anti-aircraft) each side of the octopoidal (super structure where the bridge is.) There were various anti-aircraft guns about the ship, which made her a formidable craft.

When they went ashore in Scapa Flow, there were only sheep and a large place where they could get a beer and something to eat. It had a piano in it, so they could have a singsong. Later they built a Cinema for them.

One day returning to H.M.S. Rodney, on the liberty boat. After a few pints being on shore leave. Norman was singing as he was happy and merry (not drunk). As they got alongside the Rodney and before he went up the after gangway on to the quarter deck, he stopped singing, as he knew he couldn't sing on the quarterdeck, which is holy ground. The officer of the watch had been watching the boat come alongside and had heard Norman singing and thought he was drunk so he got the quarter master to pipe "Thumping Party Lay Aft". That was a signal to thump is for Thumping anyone who is rowdy or drunk, and knock them out.

So as soon as he got on to the quarterdeck, the officer of the watch, pointed to Norman, just as he was saluting the quarterdeck. A big royal marine hit Norman on the chin, and knocked Him out. Norman came round a bit as the officer was carrying him on his shoulder along the upperdeck, going forward to the hatch, leading to the cells, which are below near the bottom of the ship. The officer dropped him down the hatch which had steel stairs down. Norman had to go down two more decks before he got to the cells. There were about four cells.

They were three ft wide, seven ft long, seven ft high. Norman's bed was two ft wide wood, with a block of wood for his pillow. So he thought, "I am not putting my head on that, I'll put my feet on it." So he took his Jumper off and used that for his pillow. He had no blanket and he tried to get some sleep. The marine had to stay outside as a sentry.

Norman didn't get much sleep as it was cold down below in the bows of the ship.

He felt tired, cold and rough.

The next day he had to see the Commander as a defaulter. He didn't give Norman any justice. All he got off him was seven days number 11 punishment. (Norman only sings in the bath now). The longest time anyone stays in the cells on the ship, is 14 days.

A longer punishment involved leaving the ship, and being sent to the Glass House. A place in Colchester, for three Months.

One time in Scapa Flow, they had plum-duff for afters at dinnertime; no one liked it, as it was too heavy to eat. So we took it to the bows of the ship, gave it broken up to the seagulls. They had so much; they couldn't fly, so they walked to the edge of the deck and jumped off and they sat on the sea.

When Norman was 20, He was then old enough to have an issue of a tot of rum. They had to put a request in for it and if they didn't want it, they got three pence a day in their pay. In shore bases, and big ships. The rum issue was, two parts of water, one part of rum. On small ships, one of water, one of rum. Petty officers and above got neat rum. The rum was issued each day at 12 noon. Petty officers got their's at 11 am. The rum had to be drawn from the rum locker half an hour before it was issued. When the rum locker was being opened an officer had to be present. No one was allowed in the locker till the fans had been on for half an hour. The fumes were very strong. The rum was in large barrels. At 10 am the quarter master pipes on the loud speakers. "Up Spirits". The crew on the Rodney used to say, "Stand-Fast the Holy Ghost.

H.M.S Nelson, Taken from H.M.S. Rodney No. 1
Night time (Sister ships) Freetown Run.

H.M.S. Nelson, Taken from H.M.S. Rodney No.2
Night time (Sister ships) Freetown Run.

CHAPTER 6

Convoy Duty

After tests and trials were over. They left Scapa for a convoy going to Freetown and Cape Town. Troop ships were on their way into Africa via the Indian Ocean. They had to have sun helmets and tropical gear as they were crossing the Equator (Not so long ago they were in the Arctic!). When they reached Cape Town and were in sight of Table Mountain, they didn't go ashore there, as the battleships, the Warspite and the Valiant, took over to take the convoy up the Indian Ocean to Africa. They went back to Freetown to wait for the next convoy. They got shore leave in Freetown (not a nice place to be in.) When they went ashore, on return they were given a quinine tablet to take against malaria. As they stepped on the ship an officer was there to see that they took it. They were sweating all the time, their pores were sore, and so they had cream to use. The natives came round with their canoes, shouting for money to be thrown in the water. They shouted "Liverpool sixpence Johnny" or "Glasgow tanner Jack". They could dive out of their canoes without tipping them up, and get the money that was thrown to them in the water. They also came with bananas, pineapples, and coconuts etc. They would trade socks, singlet's, duty free cigs, (Players sixpence for 20, woodbines 4 '/2 pence for 20). When they were in Drake Barracks they could buy cig tobacco or pipe tobacco '/z lb. tin for one shilling and three pence for rolling their own cigs. One day in Freetown a native was passing the ship in his canoe, and two cooks were throwing a sack of rubbish over the side. They didn't look to see if all was clear, so when they threw it, it landed on top of the native and his canoe. All went down, the native was mad. He got most of his stuff and put his canoe right. A pole was made for the boom that sticks out from the ship's side, with a rope ladder and wire to tie boats up, so they wouldn't bang on the ship's side. The ladder was for the boats' crews to climb up or down to get in or out of the boat. The native got on the boom to get on the ship. As the deck was hot they had hosepipes with seawater running all the time to keep the ship cool. When the native got on the boom they turned the hose full on and knocked him off it. He was mad again and said; "I'll remember Rodney when you come ashore."

The tropical routine was bathing hands at 6am, finish work at 11 am, unless on duty. The evening was best because they would have a film show on upper deck, or some music. Sometimes they had a show, other times a boxing match. They lay in our hammocks on the upper deck to sleep, as it was too hot below. Awnings (canvas sheeting) were rigged to keep the sun off. Sometimes it rained heavily in the night, so there was a °right scramble to get below and sleep first deck down.

On the first trip to Cape Town and crossing the Equator (crossing the line) because most of the crew had not crossed it before, a ceremony was arranged. Two marines dressed up as King and Queen Neptune. A canvas tank 3ft wide and 8ft long was rigged on the deck. It was about 3ft deep full of seawater. Those who had crossed before gathered round it. Those who had not crossed before were put in the tank at one end, ducked and couldn't get out till they got to the other end, being ducked as they went along. Even the commander, who was a three-ring officer, got ducked.

The crew got their own back on him, as he was always giving them lectures on damage control, in the silent hours (their time). When the ducking was over, a loud voice on the speakers said, "Stop the ship". (The ship didn't stop). Then the King and Queen Neptune came out of the forward hatch. A table and platform were rigged up. Then King Neptune was giving out knighthoods to anyone who wanted one; there was a long queue. Instead of a sword on their shoulders, he used a rubber fish. The Queen was giving kisses; the queue was longer for that. Then, there were awards. The chief writer was given a pencil two feet long. The head diver received a divers helmet full of seawater.

Walrus sea plane crossing the Equator on troop ships going to Africa via the Indian Ocean.

Troopships in convoy going to Africa via the Indian Ocean

Destroyer coming for oil with out stopping. Troopships in convoy going to Africa via the Indian Ocean.

Crossing the Equator Freetown to Cape Town nine 16" Guns

Crossing the Equator ceremony King and Queen Neptune

Crossing the Equator ceremony. King Neptune gives chief writer a pencil

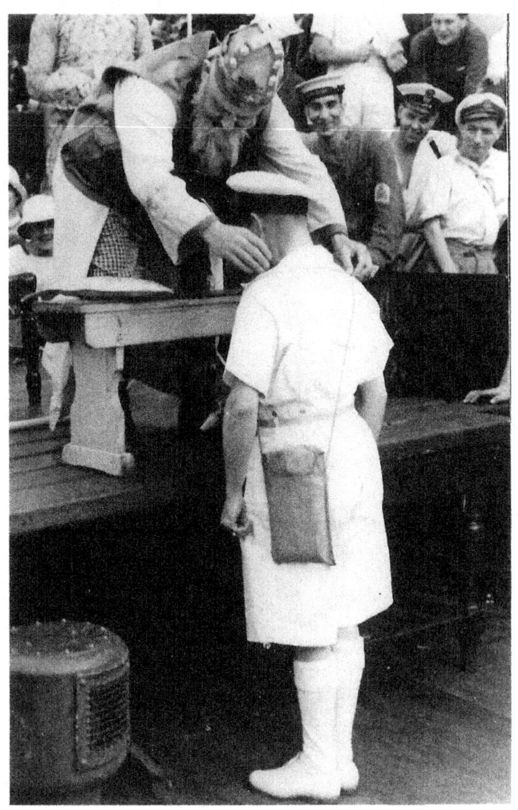

H. M. S. Nelson in Freetown taken from H.M.S. Rodney (Sister Ships)

Maltese Looking at Walrus Seaplane Off H.M.S Rodney.

The chief stoker was given a child's bucket and spade, the gunners' mate, a toy cap gun.

Then they had to get back to duty.

The commander was on the H.M.S. Ark Royal when it was sunk. During his lectures, he was always saying. "When I was on the Ark." It was decided to have a competition of making a sketch for a Crossing the Line certificate. The best one was made by G Takel So a lot were printed and given out to those who qualified. Norman had his put in a frame.

One time in harbour in Freetown, while waiting for the next convoy, they were painting the ships side. They had wooden stages to sit on. That was a plank, long enough for two to sit on; there were two cross pieces, one at each end, to keep the plank away from the ships side and make space for their legs while sitting. It also had a rope at each end to lower it. They started at the top and it was lowered, as they painted. When they got near the water, they had to get in a boat, while the stage was moved along and onto the stage by a sailor. It was very hot; so they used to fall off the stage into the sea, deliberately, to cool off, then swim to the after gangway, and on to the quarterdeck. They couldn't do that too often, or they would be punished.

The part of the ships side near the water was painted from a boat.

Streaming paravanes to cut mines loose

Malta Convoy H.M.S Nelson in background left.

They also sang this song: You take the paintbrush. I'll tale the paint pot

And we'll paint the ships side together.
When Jimmy comes along, we'll sing this little song.
Thank the Lord we never joined forever.

(Jimmy is the first lieutenant.)

One day while on the Freetown run, they had heard about the ship H.M.S. Nelson hitting a mine.

She had a big hole in the bows, so had to go into dock. They started to stream Paravanes, one each side from the bows. (A device with sharp teeth, which cut the mooring cables of submerged mines.)

They cut a few loose and then fired guns at them, s they came to the surface, to blow them up.

Gibraltar was the place we visited most, while in the Mediterranean Sea. They had some exciting runs ashore there. The first one was to have a good look round the place. The Royal Marines took Gibraltar, over 300 years ago. The airport is a strip of land that joins Gibraltar to mainland Spain. The army are in the upper most part of the rock. They look after the apes that are on the rock, and they defend it, with large guns built into the rock.

There is a dockyard with workshops and dry docks, that part is the Royal Navy's area. This has a cinema, canteen, like a pub and a football pitch of white granite, which is not good to play football on. Norman often had sore knees and elbows playing on it. The first time he went into the cinema, they played music while waiting for the show to start. There was a ledge where the roof met the walls each side. Seven or eight rats came along the ledge on each side as the music started, he thought they were going to give them a turn, as all the matelots (sailors) started clapping and cheering. When they went into the town part, there were three kinds of pubs. One was called the Royal. It had an all senoritas big band in there, and it was more select. The other two were rough dives. Trocadero had Spanish dancers giving a show and so it was full in there, and a lot of sailors got drunk. The other one was the Universal, halfway down the main street. It had no windows, just openings where windows used to be. It didn't do to walk past those openings as you might get hit by a table or chair, as many fights used to start there. It was better to cross over the street, where it was safer. Norman and his mate Alf used to go in a place, called Smokey Joes, a small place where they met some soldiers, Geordies who were based on the rock. They went up to their barracks and their canteen. They all got on well together. There were other times of a more serious nature. They had to drop small depth charges over the ship's side every quarter of an hour. To ward off frogmen putting mines on ships' bottom at night time. They sent divers down during the day to inspect all the ships' bottom.

When the war was almost over with Germany, Norman was on the base staff in Gibraltar, so was allowed to go into Spain for a day, 9am - 9pm. He had to go in civvys clothes, which he borrowed from a bloke in the R.A.F. Camp. First he had to put in a request to his officer to go. Then he had to go to the Spanish Consul, and British Consul to get papers, so he could cross the border into Spain. he went with a Sailor called David from Edinburgh. They had a good day in La Linea, a guide showed them round. They went into the bullring, but as it was a weekday, no bullfight was on. They only had them once a month on a Sunday. He told them all about it. They also went in to SanRoci; a small place, it had an archway at the entrance, which to Norman's surprise had the names of Franco, Hitler, Mussolini carved out of the white stone in blue letters.

Gibraltar had a football team, Gibraltar United. They had a very good team, some of their players were international standard. One day the Royal Navy played them. The Navy won 4-1. It was chalked all over the dockyard. Some of the sailors went out with Gibraltar girls. They had to have their mother with them as chaperone.

One day HMS Pheasant, a bird class sloop, came in for repairs in the dry dock. Norman went on board as they were about to connect to shore electricity. Norman asked for Frank Harding who is his cousin. They said, go down this hatch, walk aft, till you get to the QO's store, Norman is there. It was dark down below it just had small emergency lights on the bulkheads. he got to the QO's store. There were three sailors standing outside it. Norman asked for Frank Harding. One of them said," that's me", Norman said," come up to where I can see you, I am your cousin." They went on to the upper deck. Norman told him who he was, as they had not seen each other since they were small boys. Frank was wearing boots with no laces in. Norman said, "What's this no laces?" Norman said, "Anything happens to this ship, I would kick these Boots off, and over the side I would go."

Frank was a good swimmer, he lived near a canal. When people used to fall in when it was dark or foggy. Frank got a medal off the council for Saving a lot of lives.

They arranged to go for a drink together in the evening. Frank brought a mate with him. They went to the naval canteen and had a good night together. Then Frank's ship was off to sea again. Norman visited Frank after the war where he lived in Warrington.

Another time Norman remembered going ashore in Gibraltar. This time a sailor called Tim Cronin from Middlesbrough, asked Alf and Norman if he could go ashore with them. They said, "Ok", they went in their usual places, navy canteen, Smokey Joe's, up to the Geordies to see the soldiers they had met many times. They had a good time, but Tim was not used to what they were used to, so he got drunk. They made their way back to the place where they got a boat back to the Rodney.

There was a lot of sailors from other ships, French, Yanks, Polish, and some marines.

They had Tim between them, making their way through the crowd, to get near where their boat would come in, so they could get Tim on it safely. In doing so they bumped into some yanky sailors. One of them turned round and hit Tim in the mouth, Tim in return hit out and hit a marine off their ship, who was going to thump Tim, Alf and Norman grabbed the marine and explained what had happened, So calmed things down. A sickbay attendant who was standing near, and was off the Rodney, Said to Alf," what are you doing ashore Alf with that leg? You know you shouldn't be ashore."

While they was talking, he looked, and couldn't find Tim, he got to the end of the crowd and saw a yanky sailor had Tim on the ground, and was holding him by the throat; at that time he was passing another yanky sailor who was leaning against some guard rails. He saw that he had seen what was happening, so put his hand on Norman's shoulder and said," one at a time Bud." he gave him a forearm smash right on his Adams apple. That shut him up, he ran over to Tim and the Yank, and got hold of the Yank shouting," let go", he wouldn't so he bent down and put Norman's left hand under his chin, pulled his head round hard, then hit him as hard as he could in the face. He fell off Tim and the other Yank didn't interfere. So Norman got Tim, slung him over his shoulder, and took him back to where Alf was. Alf said, "what's happening?" Norman told him. He said, "if we get them Yanks on the catamaran for their boat the same time as ours, we will put them in the drink. (Sea)

(A catamaran was a floating platform) There boat came in first so they had to get on it.

They sorted Tim out, so all was well.

One day in harbour in Freetown West Africa, time to bathe hands at 6am. They had two wide wooden ladders on the ship's side, so two could climb each ladder side by side. This was to clear the water quickly, if the ship had to leave in a hurry. If any sharks came into the harbour. Royal Marines were on the deck with rifles there was also a bugler to sound, "clear the water."

One day the crew of a motor cutter found a dead shark when they had been to a small inlet down the coast taking non-swimmers to learn to swim. They tied a rope to the shark and towed it behind the boat, then came in the harbour with it. The bugler sounded, "clear the water;" the marines were firing at the shark. The water was cleared in record time. The boat's crew was severely punished. They use to take the non- swimmers to a sandy beach to learn to swim. Norman was one of the swimmers who was teaching them. The first time they did it, Norman dived in as they entered the inlet. Norman got the shock of his life as it was full of fish touching him all over.

Another time in Freetown, and sleeping on the upper deck near a 16" gun turret as usual, Norman woke just before reveille, and found he was the only one on the deck. It had been raining in the night, so everyone had rushed below. How they didn't stand on Norman in the rush, he will never know. Norman's hammock bedding was dry, he was under the awning, but the rain that ran down the big gun turret missed him. (Wonders never cease).

When going ashore in Freetown wearing shirts, shorts and sun helmets, it would start raining down in sheets, so they just stood there letting it cool them off. One each side of the dirt roads were ditches, they became rivers. After a few trips to Cape Town, they went home to Plymouth, their home port.

While in Plymouth they were having extra guns fitted on the ship, close range weapons. They were Oerlikonr 20mm. some twin, power mounted, most single. Wherever there was a space a gun was fitted. They had magazines that had 60 rounds in them. The 20mm shells had to be greased when being loaded into the mag. They loaded one tracer, one HE high explosive, one incendiary and so on. They also got 16" shells which were a new type to fire at torpedo bombers. They didn't know at that time, what it was all for and had to wait till they used them. When all was finished they put to sea. It was the practice of the captain to tell them where they were going, after they were a few miles out to sea. This time he didn't, Norman had passed out to be an Able seaman, so when he was on watch, he was steering the ship. There were three steering positions, the upper one, the lower one, and the after one. They usually used the lower one. They had to watch a tape with degrees on, which moved when they moved the wheel. There was a pointer, which was fixed above the tape, called the Lubbers Point. They had to get the Pointer on the degrees of the course, in which they were ordered to steer. As it was down below, orders came by voice pipe for the course to steer, from the Officer of the Watch on the bridge. They only did half an hour on the wheel at a time, and then someone else took over. It was called doing a trick. They could see a lot of ships on the horizon, so everyone was wondering what it was. They thought it was an invasion they were taking part in. When Norman went off watch, to his mess, everyone was asking him what course they were on, Norman told them, "we are not on one course, it is changing all the time." They found out they were not trying to catch the ships up. They were using them as a decoy.

It was a big convoy to Malta.

Malta convoy night attack tracer fire

Malta Convoy Stuka Dive Bomber
Shot down.

CHAPTER 7

More Convoy Duty

The enemy would think that the convoy had no protection of capital ships. The convoy was only doing 12knots. They caught it up as they entered the Mediterranean at 1 am. They could see Gibraltar lit up on our port side. No blackout at Gibraltar. They knew where they were going then. The captain told them in the morning. They could see all the ships, of a very big convoy. They were near the rear of the convoy on the port side of it, H.M.S. Rodney, and H.M.S. Nelson, on the Starboard side of the convoy. Rodney & Nelson are sister ships, that means the same, twins. About 9.30.am a plane spotted them; They were only at cruising stations. They were expecting trouble soon. That day after Norman had had his dinner it was about 12.30pm, he went for some fresh air onto the upper deck. He was looking at all the ships in this big convoy. 14 merchant ships in the Centre, seven Cruisers, making a ring round the merchant ships. Towards the rear aircraft carriers, some fleet aircraft carriers, some utility aircraft carriers, they were made just for transporting planes, in this case, Spitfires for the defence of Malta. Then 24 destroyers making a ring round the whole convoy. This would be about 20 miles wide; ships needed plenty of room to manoeuvre. The Rodney was the flagship; we had a rear admiral on board. All signallers on all ships had to watch the flag ship for a signal. When the signal was done by flags up the mast. The signaller on the flag ship hoists the flags up the mast, but stops short of the top. That is called at the dip. All other ships put the same flags at the dip, on their ships, when the signaller on the flag ship sees all have got the signal (He is on the bridge). He shouts the signal to the Officer of the Watch, and runs the flags to the top of the mast. All the other ships carry out the order all at the same time. This is very important when the order is to zig- zag. Ships moving to the left then right continually and in time with the flag ship, so as they don't collide with each other.

Malta convoy H.M.S. Eagle torpedoed.

Malta Convoy.

As Norman was watching the convoy, an Aircraft Carrier H.M.S. Eagle was doing 35 knots into the wind, as she had planes taking off; there were four or five in the sky. All of a sudden, there were four loud bangs, The Eagle had been hit by four torpedoes and she started to lean over right away and men and planes slid into the sea. Norman watched her go down; she was gone in seven minutes. The flags and order to zig zag went up right away. And action stations were sounded on the bugle and on the loud speakers. Norman thought we haven't started yet, as he knew we would get, dive bombers, torpedo bombers, U boats, E boats, attacking for a week, so Norman thought, "I'm not going to get out of the Mediterranean alive."

Malta convoy H.M.S. Eagle sinking, hit by four torpedoes.

Malta convoy ships stopped after near miss, crew abandoned. Royal Navy Sloop, tells crew to get back on board.

Malta convoy - Stuka Dive Bomber diving at H. M. S. Rodney

Malta convoy aircraft carrier H. M. S. Indomitable damaged, returning for repairs after convoy going to Gibraltar. Taken from H.M.S. Rodney.

Malta convoy near miss

Ships under attack
Malta Convoy

The Planes in the sky from H.M.S. Eagle, had to land on the other fleet aircraft carriers. Norman then had to get to his action station, which was the starboard wing magazine, B turret. They knew at dusk and dawn they would have torpedo bombers attacking, that is the best time for them to attack. They would then know whether the new type 16" shells would be successful. A 16" shells had never been fired at aircraft before. They couldn't fire at dive bombers or high level aircraft, only at low flying planes like torpedo bombers. They attacked in fives till we shot a few down, then they came in ones. In the magazine which had a loud speaker, when the Air Defence Officer said," Stand by Starboard", (on his mike), torpedo bombers were approaching on the starboard beam. They were in the starboard beam mag. All six of them were saying their prayers. One of the six came from Wigan; he was always saying he was an atheist. He soon changed his mind when he thought a torpedo was coming in at them. If a torpedo had hit, they would have all been blown to bits. The Rodney shot 27 torpedo bombers down with 16" shells. History in the making. The convoy was called (Operation Pedestal) (The Maltese called it the "Santa Maria Convoy" as it was August 10th 1942.)

(And the 11th, 12th, 13th, 14th, and the time of the Annunciation made by the Angel Gabriel to Mary.) The convoy had to get to Malta no matter what the cost. Out of 14 merchant ships four got there. aircraft carrier H.M.S. Eagle sank. The aircraft carrier Indomitable badly damaged. The cruiser Manchester sank. cruiser Cairo, sank, cruiser Kenya was badly damaged. The destroyer Foresight, sank. The oil tanker "Ohio" was torpedoed and holed, an exploding stuka crashed on her deck, her boilers blew up and her engines failed. She was twice abandoned and twice reboarded. repeated attempts to tow her failed. She would not sink. With her decks awash, she was lashed between two destroyers and led into Grand Harbour with her precious cargo on the 15th August which was the Feast of the Assumption. The Rodney then made her way to Gibraltar escorting the badly damaged carrier Indomitable, Which had a lot of wounded on board. So she signalled to Rodney to increase speed to 30 knots. Rodney replied, "What are you going to do, take us in tow?" Carriers can do 35 knots to enable the planes to fly off. Rodney could do about 22 knots. When they got into Gibraltar, (it was August 16th 1942), the order over the loud speakers was "Hands to make and mend", that means you can do what you like, you can do your washing, see to your kit, write letters, or get your hammock up, get in it and go to sleep. Most of the crew did that this time, as they had no sleep for over a week. Norman found when he got in his hammock about 9pm. he was so tense; he didn't go to sleep till about 4am. Then it was reveille at 6.30am. He had to get up again. Some who were on duty didn't get a Make and Mend, till next day, or when they came off watch.

After a few days in Gibraltar. They went back to Scapa, after a few days there they went to Rosyth Naval Dockyard Scotland, for repairs, on 22°d August. As they had to go under the Forth Railway Bridge, they had to strike down the main mast to get under it, (some job that was). They then got some welcome leave, seven days. The first party went on leave at midnight. They had to go through a large hut, inside was the customs, so a lot was worried, they may have too many duty free cigs, or anything else they would have to pay duty on. The entrance was a blackout door, so they looked in to see what was happening. They were searching every other ones case, so they tried to be the one that was missed. Norman's mate Bill Savage was a few in front of him as they went through the hut, he was missed, so he was counting the ones in front of Norman and it looked as if he was going to be searched, there were three customs officers doing the job, they were all busy as he passed through, and he was missed. Norman found Bill, in the dark outside. They then had to wait for another pal a scouser. We waited a while. He didn't come, so they thought he had was caught. He finally came; he was looking all over in the dark. "What are you looking for?" Norman asked him. He had a lot of duty free cigs, over the amount. So he had, got them out of his case and tied them up in a bath towel. Then thrown them right over the hut. Lucky he found them in the dark. There was a train in the dockyard waiting for them all. They got on it and were waiting for the rest or the party to get on. They were congratulating themselves at getting away with the loot. When a buzz (rumour) went along the train that they (customs) were going to search again. What a panic that started, they were putting stuff on top of the train, under it, anywhere they could find, until they found out it was a false alarm. The one who started it would have been lynched if they had caught him. All went ok, and the train moved off to take the crew on leave with a smiling face on board.

Churchill visited H.M.S. Rodney before the invasion of North Africa to give them a pep talk.

He had Sir Stafford Cripps with him, also three body guards, dressed like chauffeurs, and some high ranking Naval officers. Two Army officers were also present. They came to discuss with the Naval officers (gunnery) about the crew shelling the coast, before the soldiers went in, at North Africa.

Churchill meets captain with Sir Stafford Cripps in Scapa Flow

Churchill giving a pep talk before the invasion of North Africa on H.M.S. Rodney in Scapa Flow

On H.M.S. Rodney, Churchill meets the sailors in Scapa Flow. Before invasion of North Africa.

Malta Convoy Night Attack Tracer Fire

CHAPTER 8

September 1942 (Operation Torch)

After repairs to damage near the stem and rudder caused by a near miss from enemy aircraft while on the Malta convoy, the crew and all returned from leave. Rodney left the United Kingdom on convoy duty bound for the invasion of North Africa. Their first job was to bombard the shore positions with 16" shells. A large African Hawk perched on the end of one of the 16" Gun barrels, while it was in the horizontal position for loading. Norman was on the bridge and he thought it would fly off when the gun went up for firing. It didn't, as the gun fired and flames and shell left the gun, the bird was cremated and the suction of the shell leaving the gun caused it to follow so far then plummet into the sea. Three French destroyers came out to stop the crew. One was set on fire, one had its forward gun knocked overboard by a 16" shell, the other one went back in harbour quickly. So the crew had no trouble shelling the shore batteries. After a while the captain decided to use 6" guns, so the crew had to move in closer to get the range, they only fired a few rounds 6" and as they came in the range of the shore batteries. They put two shots in front of the crew's bows, two shots near their stern, two short and two over the top. So it was, hard for starboard and get out of their range, and back on 16". When the shore Batteries were silenced, their next job was to knock out a Fort Santon, which was stopping the American army advancing. The crew couldn't see the Fort from the sea, so they had to have their seaplane a Walrus.

Walrus sea plane being catapulted off during shelling of Fort Santon, In North Africa.

H.M.S. Rodney firing 16" guns shelling North Africa coastal defences

A Walrus catapulted off, to go and spot where the 16" shells were landing. This was done with great success, so after a few days, the Fort capitulated. The American army advanced with very little trouble. The crew used a port called Mers -el-Kebir. While in that harbour, one night a plane dropped something in the water they didn't know what it was until there was a loud explosion. A merchant ship had been hit by a torpedo. It was a new type which, after it landed it started to circle round and round until it hit something. So the crew had to have wire nets with balls on keeping the net afloat. Two motor cutters had each end of the net. So when they dropped these things, the motor cutters wrapped the net round it and towed it out of the harbour to sea. After so far out they'd let it go. It was a while before the crew got any shore leave in Mers-el-Kebir.

The first time Norman went ashore in Oran, North Africa. he went with his regular shore going mate Alf. They landed at Mers-el-Kebir, and then got a lift in a jeep from the yanks, to Oran. What a ride, the jeep went round the bends on two wheels and they were glad to get off it. They only had a short time ashore, from 12.30pm, they had to be back on board by 6pm. They went for a drink in Oran, They only had French beer, not like English beer, they didn't like it, they were watching a French man standing at the bar, he had a very small glass, which must have contained wine. He just had a sip. The crew thought they would try it, they didn't sip it, as they were used to drinking beer, so they tried a few types, and downed them in two drinks. After a few Norman said to Alf, "let's get out of here, Norman can feel this stuff getting hold of him" and he agreed. So they got drunk. Alf was a stocky bloke, also quiet, until he had a few drinks. Then he wanted to fight everyone. They met some yanks, who said, "are you limies?"

The crew said, "Yes we are limies". The yanks said, and "We don't like limies", the crew said, "We don't like yanks," so a fight started. The area they were in was near the bottom of some steps and dirt road wet and muddy. Norman was knocked backwards down the stone steps, hit his head on one of them and finished in the wet mud, he was out for the count. The yanky M.Ps, came, couldn't bring Norman round and so he was taken to the hospital in Oran.

It was a French hospital, taken over by the Americans. Norman was then 20 years of age, wearing shorts and shirt, which got in a right mess. he came round at 9.30 am having been out since about 2 pm yesterday. Norman was shocked to find himself in hospital, he had a bad headache when he went to sit up. The man in the next bed said, "Don't sit up bud, You've got a fractured skull!" That shocked Norman more. There was no one in the bed on his right, the yank on his left was called Gustov, and he was Italian nationalised American. He was in a cave during the invasion, which collapsed in on him, so was going back to America as soon as he was well enough. Opposite Norman was six black Americans. One of them had a fractured skull; he had fits now and then, during one of them, he tried to get in the bed, of the one on his right, who had been in a crash in a jeep, who now was better and going back to duty soon, which caused an uproar. Some of the yanks played cards on Gustov's bed with him, a game called Peaknockel which they played for money. The black yank who had been in the jeep crash, also played and they used to cheat him. He would find out and say, "I think you're cheating me." One night after 9.30pm, which was lights out, Gustov got out of bed and crept across the ward, put his hand under the bed clothes of the jeep yank. He thought it was the one next to him having a fit again, so he fell out of bed the other side, on to the floor, got up and ran out of the ward. The entire ward was laughing, and the jeep man came back and said to Gustov, "Don't do that Gus, I'm scared, I'm scared of ghosts." Norman was in hospital a few weeks, and then was taken to a convalescent camp, what a dump; it was where the invasion had taken place. There were no doors or windows in the building, a folding canvass bed, one blanket. Norman's clothes were in a mess. The yanks ditched them and gave Norman their uniform. It was cold at night, so everyone kept their clothes on. After a week, Norman had to see the doctor, so Norman asked him, "Could I go back to my ship?" He said, "No, you will be here for two more weeks yet." One day a lorry came in the camp. The driver said to Norman, "Your ship is in Mers-el- Kebir." It was about 10am. Norman thought, "I am getting on that somehow." A lorry was taking some yanks to Oran, so he would have to pass Mers-el-kebir, so Norman got on the back end of it, as he was wearing their uniform, no one said anything. When it got to Mers-el-Kebir.

Norman could see the Liberty boat 12.30pm. crossing the harbour. He shouted, "Stop, I'm getting off'. They banged on the front of the cab, so it stopped. Norman got off and went down to the jetty, as the Liberty Boat came alongside. Some men who knew Norman said, "What are you doing? Have you joined the American Army?" Norman said, "Have I heck," they said," You must have, you're wearing their uniform," Norman said, "I am getting on this boat and I don't want to miss it, I'll tell you about it later". When they got to the Rodney and Norman got on to the quarter deck, the Officer of the Watch, said, "Who are you? What are you doing on here?" Norman explained to him who he was and had just come out of hospital.

He said, "Go to the sick bay and report to the Surgeon Commander." When Norman saw the Surgeon Commander, he said, "Where are your discharge papers off the hospital?" Norman said, "They didn't give me any". He examined Norman and said. "I am keeping you under observation, you must stay in the sick bay, don't leave it." After a while he left the sick bay. So Norman asked the sick bay attendant, "Could I go to my mess and get my own clothes and get out of this American gear?" He said, "You know what he said, you have to stay in here, he will be in trouble if he let you go." Norman said, "I won't be long. he won't be back yet". "OK" he said, "but don't be long." Norman went to his mess, everyone was looking at him and thinking what is this American doing on the ship. Those who knew Norman, wanted to know why, he was in a hurry and he had no time to talk to anyone. When Norman got to his mess, he found his locker was empty. Norman went to see his Divisional Officer, who said, "Hello Moors are you OK now?" Norman told him he was in the sick bay, He said, "Your kitbag and hammock are on H.M.S. Vindictive. It's a cruiser, which is in the harbour. He will get a boat and someone to carry your kitbag and hammock; you will have to see the Master at Arms and sign for things".

Norman went with two seamen in the boat, got to the Vindictive; Norman saw the Master at Arms signed for everything. He got to the after gangway where the boat was, then blacked out and tumbled down the steps and into the boat. Norman came round in the boat and was not too bad, he had a few bumps and grazes and he had torn his trousers right up his leg. Norman got back on the Rodney OK.

Norman took a pair of overalls out of his kitbag. The seaman put Norman's gear in his locker and hammock in the rack. Norman then went back to the sick bay.

The attendant blew his top and said, "Don't you dare leave here again! Good job the Surgeon Commander has not been back, or you would have been in the Rattle (punishment)". The ship went out of Mers-el-Kebir, was patrolling the North African part of the Med.

After about two weeks, Norman was back on duty, then after a month, the ship went into Mers-el-Kebir again. They hadn't been there long, when the Surgeon Commander sent for Norman. He said, "What do you think you are playing at Moors?, I've had a signal off the American Army wanting to know of your whereabouts, as you are reported missing and they have a warrant for your arrest. They are looking for you in Oran." Norman explained the reason why he left the convalescent camp and that he wanted to be back on the ship, he said that he saw the chance, when he was told the ship was back in Mers-el-Kebir and he saw the Liberty Boat coming ashore, so he got on it. The commander said, "I will send a reply to this signal, saying you are now back on board and in good health and thank them for looking after you but if they want to take this matter further, you will be in serious trouble". Norman then went back to his duty. The Americans didn't bother, so he was very lucky, he got off Scot free. After that he never went ashore again with Alf.

The group of ships that were in the North Africa campaign were called Force H. That consisted of (H.M.S Rodney, H.M.S. Nelson, Battleships) H.M.S. Indomitable, an aircraft carrier, some destroyers. Other ships joined the group from time to time, H.M.S. Jamaica a cruiser.

The next job after knocking out the fort Santon was escorting a troop convoy to Algiers. Norman's brother David, a soldier was on that convoy, Norman didn't know at the time, but David knew he was on the Rodney. While patrolling in the Med one night, what looked like two planes coming towards them, with a light on each of them, turned out to be a plane guiding a remote controlled bomb. Before they knew it, it hit the aircraft carrier H.M.S. Indomitable, on the flight deck. The plane guiding it made off before it could be fired at. The carrier had to go to Gibraltar for repairs. The next time one of these bombs was chasing the Nelson at its stern. The Nelson was going as fast as it could, and firing everything at the bomb. It got a hit and blew up the bomb. After that was invasion of Sicily, so they had to bombard the coast, and knock the shore batteries out, before the soldiers went in. Then they had some shore leave in Malta. The people there were very short of food. The crew gave them what they could and children came on board with white enamel buckets for any food left over, after their meals. They were called "Gash Boys". The crew gave them cigs, anything they could such as sweets and chocolate. The next job was invasion of Italy. They entered the Messina Straits near Reggio and Bombarded the coastal defences. That took them about two days, before the soldiers went in. They then patrolled the area, a few planes were attacking but Force H sustained no damage. After a while the soldiers advanced well into Italy. After that was Salerno. On September 7th the beachhead was established so the assault convoys could land on the 9th. On the 8th Force H was attacked by torpedo carrying aircraft. None of their ships was damaged, though Warspite and Formidable had near misses. The anti aircraft fire of the force was effective, three aircraft were shot down and three more were thought to be destroyed. The force including Rodney maintained patrol of the seas off West Coast of Italy. The next target was the Anzio Beachhead, which was near Rome. All went well with no trouble for the navy. After a few days patrolling, they returned to Malta. Then it was homeward bound for Plymouth, in time to get leave for Christmas 1943. Norman was lucky to be on the Christmas Party. Others were on the New Year Party. (7 days leave).

In Malta aircraft carrier H.M.S. illustrious. Norwegian war ship H. M. S Rodney

Malta Convoy Night Attack Tracer Fire

Norman's first day on leave was a visit to a pal he had while in the Boys Brigade - Joe Maddocks. They went to a pub called the Radnor. It had a large room and stage for entertainment. They were at the bar having a drink and a chat when Joe noticed two girls, sat at a table. Joe said, "I know those two girls, sat at the table. Let's wait and see if they are with anyone." After a while no one looked to be with them. So they walked over to them and Joe said, "hello", and introduced Norman to them. They sat down and Norman was sitting next to Nancy and Joe was sitting next to Doris. They got talking and Nancy said she was 21, the same age as Norman. She also said she was a twin, the same as Norman. They got on fine and Norman found her easy to talk to. The next night they all went to a cinema and had a drink. As they were walking home, Joe and Doris were in front(a few yards). They were talking to each other, then Nancy said, "Can't we go out on our own tomorrow?" I said, "Yes, if you want." So she said she would like to. Norman shouted to Joe, "Nancy and I are going out on our own tomorrow okay?" He said, "Okay if you want."

So he said to Nancy he would call for her at 7pm the next day.

Norman called at her house at 7pm the next day and we got on fine and he had a good leave. On the way back, he did a lot of thinking about the future. Norman thought this is it, he will now have earn more money, and pick up his trade as a fitter engineering, for when the war is over. Norman had done four years apprenticeship out of a seven year one, so he was three years short. Norman went to see his officer when he got back to the Rodney, and explained his position. The officer said, "You are best going into ordnance. First you will have to do a gunnery course as a QR3 and you will have to pass that, before you can go in for Ordnance. You can do the gunnery course on the ship, but can't do the ordnance on the ship. That's a dockyard job. So you had better leave the ship and go into the barracks." After a few days and the officer had made the arrangements and Norman went into barracks. It was a common practice, that if you entered the barracks, after leaving a ship you got seven days leave, right away. So he put his kitbag and hammock in the baggage store and went on seven days leave. Norman surprised everyone when he got home again. "What are you doing home again? You have only just gone back," everyone was saying. Nancy was delighted when Norman told her he had left the ship and was going to earn more money, and be able to pick up his trade again, after the war. Norman went to the barracks and he had another good seven days leave. Norman went back and passed the gunnery course and he got another seven days leave for passing the course. Norman started the ordnance course, which was harder and longer in the dockyard and he passed it. He got another seven days leave as a reward. Norman went back to wait for a draft to wherever they wanted to send him. It was the near end of March 1944. Norman got a draft abroad somewhere, and seven days embarkation leave.

CHAPTER 9

Getting Married

When Norman got home he told Nancy that he was going abroad somewhere, he didn't know where and he didn't know when he would be back. Nancy said," Lets get married." Norman said, "We will have to talk about that." Norman told Nancy that he didn't mind getting married and said, "But we are not starting a family, till the war was over. I am not taking any chance of a child having no father or no mother, or no mother and father, as we both could get killed." Nancy agreed. So Norman told Nancy's mother and father that they were getting married. They were very happy about it. Norman went with Nancy to see my parents. They tried to talk Norman out of getting married. They said Norman was too young (he was 21) and didn't know what he was doing.

We had to get married by special licence. It was at St. James Church, Moss Side, Manchester, on Wednesday April 5th 1944. All were invited but none of Norman's family came. His best man was Nancy's cousin, Harry Roberts a sailor who was on leave. The Manchester Evening News took a photo of them. It's the only photo he had. Norman sent a telegram, to ask for more leave and got one back, that was not granted.(It was a good wedding), but Norman had to go back on the Friday April 7th 1944 on the midnight train to Plymouth, then he went on a troop ship, after the ship was a few miles out to sea, he was told he was going to be on the base staff ordnance at Gibraltar.

The food was not so good on the troop ship. Better on Navy ships. It took about a week to get to Gibraltar. Norman settled into his billet the first day and then he had to report to the gun mounting shop in the dockyard the next day. A C.P.0 Artificer 2nd Class was in charge. There were two PO Artificers 4th Class, one leading hand 5th Class, then Norman Able Seaman QO, QR3. They had to go on ships that had no ordnance staff on board, to do repairs and sight tests on the guns. They worked mostly on destroyers and corvettes. The first day they set off to work on a number of ships, as they walked along the dockyard, Norman was with the leading hand. The two PO's were in front the POs walked very fast. The leading hand Norman was with walked very slowly. They got to the ships, which were tied up to each other. So they had to cross a few, before they got to the one they wanted. Norman was in front of the 50` Class man. he noticed as he crossed the ships that the one they were going to had an ape on board. The two PO's were already on the ship which was a destroyer. As Norman stepped on board, the ape had its back towards him. One of the crew slapped the ape from behind on its ear. The ape turned round very angry and the sailor pointed to Norman and the ape came jumping towards him. The ape had Norman's back to the guardrails. The ape stopped right in front of him, jumping and growling. Norman thought if he tried to move to the right or left, and showed fear, he would encourage it to attack. So he would have to stand still and look it straight in the eyes. Norman did and was tensed up ready to defend himself. After a short while, they all started laughing. The other two PO's who had rushed to get on the ship had set it all up for Norman, he wasn't laughing. Norman was very angry and told them what he thought of them all.

CHAPTER 10

Joined H. M. S. Killmartin

Norman enjoyed the work on the ships for a few months unil one day a ship, an American corvette with their navy crew on board, HMS Killmartin, had an accident on the forward gun. The gun was in semi-automatic position. After they had fired the first round, when the man loading the second round, the gun fired on its own, as it was stuck in the firing position. The man loading missed the recoil, but got the hot brass cylinder in his face, so was taken to hospital. Norman was sent onto the ship, as part of the crew and, to sort out the faulty gun. he found they had been painting, and had painted the shafts which go from the gunlayer's foot pedal to the breach firing mechanism causing the gun to stick in the firing position. he soon sorted that out, checked it a lot after that. It was a 3-50 QF gun with a vertical sliding breach. It wasn't a good gun. It was American. The other guns on board were four orlicans, two twin bofors at the stern. They had bunks to sleep in three tiers. Norman had a bottom one. Americans don't have hammocks. The bunk space was second deck down with wooden lockers for kit. The mess deck was first deck for meals and living quarters. It also had depth charges, and Hedgehog bombs (small depth charges) in a pack of ten. They mostly did eight days patrol of the Straits of Gibraltar, to catch U-Boats coming in and out of the Med.

Crew of H. M.S. Killmartin taken on the jetty at Gibraltar.

Churchill coming on board H.M.S. Rodney
In Scapa Flow

Sometimes they did slow convoy duty along the West African coast. Norman was coxswain of the liberty boat from time to time. There was a man in the bows to watch out for floating objects; he had a powerful light at night time. There was a stoker on the engines and Norman had to signal to him by bell, for slow full ahead or astern and stop One night while crossing the harbour the last boat for liberty men, and going full speed, they hit something. Norman felt it rub along the keel and thought the propellers would be damaged.

Norman shouted to the bow man," have we got a hole in the bows," he said," No". Norman stopped the engine, looked over the side. The propellers were Ok, they had a brass bar protecting them. Norman went to pick up the liberty men. One was very drunk, so when they got back alongside the ship. Norman got a long rope, and made a bowline on a boat, sat him in it and threw the rope up to his mates and told them to heave him up, and get him down below, before the officer saw him. When on patrol and chasing U-boats some of the crew would go into the Spanish waters and ports, so they could not follow them. They had two dogs on board, one a pup, also a monkey, which was on a long lead. The pup and monkey played together. The dog didn't like it when they went to sea. The captain and gunner's mate had a parakeet each in their cabins. One day while in port, the monkey got in their cabins, via the portholes and bit the heads off the parakeets. The monkey was put ashore very quickly.

CHAPTER 11

War With Germany Ends

The war with Germany ended. VE day was a great day in Gibraltar, fireworks, dancing and singing. The crew had to round U-boats up before they made for home.

The crew went through the Bay of Biscay on the way home. They didn't go that way during the war because of U-boats based at Brest, France. They were in a storm, which lasted four days. Being a small ship they had to ride out the storm. A lot was sea sick and that was the first time Norman had seen people with green faces. Norman felt bad but wasn't sick. One sailor was very bad and Norman tried to help him. He wouldn't eat his dinner or drink his rum. Norman told him he must eat, and have something in his stomach to bring up or he would strain his stomach, and not be going on leave when they got in, he would be in hospital. Norman made him a round of toast and told him to eat that dry. It took him an hour to eat it. Then he wanted a drink. Norman told him he could only have a sip of water. A bit at a time or he would start being sick again. He complained a lot, but he had to put up with it. They finally got into Sheerness and dropped anchor up the river. Norman went on shore leave at Chatham. Norman couldn't get a bed for the night and missed the last boat back to the ship, so Norman got in a small boat tied up at the jetty. It was covered in at the stern. Norman got inside and lay down on the padded form and he was soon asleep. when he woke up it was dark and he felt something on his chest; he was lying on his back and he put his hand up slowly to feel what it was and it was a cat and Norman felt cold but the cat wasn't it was purring. After a while Norman said, "Sorry puss, I'll have to disturb you as I am going for a walk, you can stay here." So Norman walked up and down the jetty till the boat came to pick the shore men up. The Americans came to take over their ship and the crew went back to the Barracks.

H. M. S. Killmartin American corvette on loan

Crew of H. M. S. Killmartin

Crew of H. M. S. Killmartin two dogs and one monkey.

Churchill meets the Officers.

CHAPTER 12

H.M.S Drake Barracks Routine

As the crew entered H.M.S, Drake Barracks, they all got seven days' leave as per practice. After returning from leave, Norman had to get used to barracks routine, which wasn't so nice, so after a few weeks of that, Norman got a draft to an Aircraft Carrier H.M.S. Illustrious, which was being repaired in the Naval dockyard at Rosyth, Scotland. Norman had a long weekend leave from Friday to Monday. Japanese Suicide Planes crashed the ship. When repaired, it was going out to the Pacific to fight the Japs again. When Norman returned from leave, he was told his draft was cancelled, as they were extending the refit. Norman had to wait for another draft, which was in two weeks time. Norman was told he was going to Miena Camp, a Naval Base in Colombo, Ceylon. It was Friday morning when Norman was told he could have a weekend leave. So he did the routine and got his pass, ticket and money and was all set to go and get the train at 1. 10 pm, when he heard on the loud speakers, "All Miena Draft will fall in at 08.30 in the morning." That was Saturday Norman would be home then. Norman asked some of his ex- ship mates, to find out what was happening at the Draft Office. Norman couldn't go near it, as they would stop his leave. They said the draft was going early. It was supposed to be going on a Tuesday. Norman had leave till the Monday. So Norman thought, " I am going on leave, if they stop me at the gate that's fair enough. So he went, showed his pass, got out and got the bus to Plymouth North Road Station. Caught the train and he was home for about 10.30pm. Norman expected to receive a telegram but didn't. Norman returned on Monday and reported to the Draft Office He was asked, "Where have you been". Norman said, "On leave here is my pass". They said, "You have missed the draft, it went on Sunday. You're on the foreign pool for the next draft."

H. M. S. Bryony Flower Class corvette.

Churchill meets the Royal Marines

CHAPTER 13

War Ends With Japan

The war with Japan ended, so Norman was taken off the Foreign Pool. Norman's next job was to go to Dartmouth where there were a lot of Flower Class corvettes, which were being sold to other countries to be used as fishing boats.

Norman was to work with a 3rd Class Artificer taking the guns off, putting them in packing cases, greasing and itemising all parts. The artificer was 35, a Welshman from Swansea. Norman was 23, from Manchester. Norman found h the welsh man didn't know how to strip the orlicans, so, Norman told him he would do them, the \welshman said, no he would do them. Norman said, "Be careful as some parts are spring loaded, so don't start pulling pins out or parts will shoot out and fall in the River Dart." That worried him sick and he tried to cover everything with his body. Norman was laughing his socks off, but didn't let him know. It was Christmas 1945; he wanted New Years leave and that suited Norman fine, as he also wanted Christmas leave.

As Taff was the only C.P.O. on the ship, when the coxswain was going on Christmas leave. Taff had to do his job. The crew gave him a hard time. He was using the coxswains cabin. When they went ashore at Christmas into Dartmouth, they were all three sheets to the wind, (drunk) So Taff went to the mess up forward, and said, "I am the coxswain now, so pipe down you lot and get in your hammocks." A scotish seaman got the bread knife out of the mess shelf and ran at Taff with it (only larking).

Taff was off to the coxswains cabin as fast as he could, he got in it and locked the door. They banged on the door putting fear into poor Taff. Norman was told all about it when he got back. All the ships were done, apart from the ammunition in the magazine. Norman had to go on them and take the temperature and enter it in the log book. There was one ship with the Chinese on board, using it as a gunnery training ship. The crew had to wait until they left. When they left, they had to go on board and strip the guns. So one morning Taff and Norman got the tools and lowered them into a boat, which was alongside the outer ship. All they had to do was drift along with the tide, till they reached the next three corvettes, and were alongside the one they wanted to get on board. The corvettes were in threes, tied to a buoy at bows and stern, so making a long line in the middle of the River Dart. The river was a 9-knot current. They got alongside the corvette. Norman got hold of the porthole, which was open, he told Taff to hold the boat to the ships side, by the porthole, while he climbed onto the ship, and then to get some rope and tie the boat up. Norman started to climb, he was standing on the edge of the boat and could just reach the top of the ships side and was about to heave himself up, when Taff started to let the boat move away from the ships side. Norman shouted, "Pull the boat in, what are you doing?" He then let go, so Norman had to jump back into the boat. He was very angry, "We will have to row back now." Taff said, "I can't row." Norman said, "You will have to learn now" he said, "You get that oar on the port side; I will get the one on the starboard side." Norman tried to show him, Taff would not lean forward enough, and pull hard, so he was turning the boat round. Norman said, "Shape yourself and pull hard on the oar." Taff said, "Let's have a rest." "Rest?" \Norman said, "You haven't done nothing yet," It was hopeless. They were drifting down to sea. They were lucky, there were some private yachts anchored, and could not be used during the war. So Norman steered the boat alongside one of them, and tied up. There was landing craft, going up and down the river, so Norman shouted to one of them. They towed them back to the corvette. They used the landing craft after that. They finished the Chinese ship. Then Norman had to wait to go back to H.M.S. Drake for demob. he was waiting about two months, before he could get sent to H.M.S. Drake Barracks for demob, as the officer said he would have to have a relief, before he could go.

Norman finally got to barracks, he was there a few days, and then was sent to H.M.S. Impregnable which was just across the river from the barracks. It was a signal training school, which had been closed, and converted into a demob camp. While Norman was there they had a large canteen with a piano in it. So they had a few good sing songs with it. Russ Conway played it. He was on radio and TV in later years. Also David Whitfield was one of the singers; he also was on radio and TV after demob. Both had been in the Navy. Russ Conway had a finger missing. Food and beer were good. They had a medical and were measured for a suit and obtained ration tickets, money and a railway ticket home.

Churchill giving pep talk on H.M.S. Rodney
Before invasion of North Africa in
Scapa Flow.

Churchill Leaving.

H.M.S. Prince of Wales
Taken from H.M.S. Rodney.

H.M.S. Killmartin
American Corvette on loan.

H.M.S. Killmartin at Anchor
African Coast.

Crew of H.M.S. Killmartin

CHAPTER 14

Civvy Street

It was April 1946 when Norman arrived in Manchester at his mother-in-law's in Moss Side. There were the hugs and kisses, cups of tea and chats; he got dressed up in his demob suit. The next day, they all went down to the pub to celebrate. Norman had six weeks leave. After only had two weeks leave Norman started work. Norman had only done four years as an apprentice fitter, so he was three years short of completing a seven year one. Norman had to see the union A.E.U. and get a firm to take him on. The firm would only have to pay half his wages and the government paid the other half. The union took into account, what Norman had been doing in the navy. They said he would have to do nine months, doing fitting at an engineering firm. Then he would be classed as a skilled fitter. Norman got a job at Locket & Croslands, who made engraving machines and embossing machines. The pay was £5 and 2 shillings a week which was 48 hours. The jobs you did had a time allocation and if you did them in less time you got a bonus. Norman had to get a tool kit together and toolbox. Norman also needed a bike to go to work on. He had a good bike before he went in the navy. A Rudge-Whitworth and Norman had asked his brother George to look after it for him. When Norman went to his mother's house to get it, in Old Trafford, it was in the cellar. It was rusty and parts missing from it. Norman's brother George who is five years older than him and didn't go into the forces, who had taken parts from it for his bike. Norman went to see him and took the bike which wanted a lot doing to it, sorted it out, and so was ready for work. Norman was then starting his Civvy life from scratch.

CHAPTER 15

First Job In Civvy Street

Norman started work at Locket & Croslands, he worded a week in hand. Norman got stuck in to it, to earn some bonus. he was making parts of a pantograph engraving machine. Norman didn't know anyone, so worked from buzzer to buzzer none stop. When he got his first pay packet after a fortnight, he looked to see what bonus he had earned. It was 14 shillings. One of the fitters who had been there a while asked me what bonus he had made. he said 14 shillings. You did well he said, not many get more than 14 shillings. he was disappointed, he thought, "I am not working that hard for 14 shillings. You were paid on a Friday after they clocked out. If there was anything wrong with your pay, you had to sort it out Saturday morning. Saturday working hours were 8am to 12 noon. If you were paid short, you had to wait till next pay packet and that happened very often.

Norman had a timesheet for his bonus. So he kept check on every job and time he did, when he knew how things were at that firm. he got a £1.00 bonus most weeks after that but, always had to wait till next week for it as it was always wrong.

After he had been there nine months and had become fed up with the place. One morning he was working on some diamond holders for a pantograph engraving machine and he had fifty to do, Norman had to file the slots that held the diamond brackets and the holders were castings, and had hard bits of metal in them. The file had to be a thin one and it soon wore out with the hard bits of metal. So he went to the stores, two floors up to get a new one. They had none, he saw the foreman on that floor, near a bench talking to a fitter, so he told him he wanted another job, as the file was worn out and stores had none. An old file was on the bench near him and he threw it along the bench to Norman, and said, "Try that." Norman looked at it, it was worn out and he threw it back to him and said, "That's no good." |Norman said "I am fed up with you, you are getting more bonus than any other fitter in the shop, and the jobs you do are not right, and someone else has to do them." That made Norman mad. So he said, "You have to pass my jobs before I get any bonus off them. What are you doing passing my jobs if they are wrong?" "There are six units of a mill engraving machine on the floor near my bench which I had done, and you have passed them and I have had the bonus off them. We will go to my bench inspect the units and if wrong and can be put right, I will put them right for free, and you will deduct the bonus I have had off them." Norman went back to his bench to wait for him. He came but didn't look at the units. He looked at the diamond holders. He got two of them; saw the hard metal in them. Then took them for heat treatment. Gave Norman them back, said, "try them." he said, "I still want a new file. Also there is fifty not two, I want another job. I am not messing about like this and I am losing money." The foreman walked away. So Norman sat on the bench. He came back, so Norman said, "I am leaving today, so have my cards and money ready by 5.30pm." Of the foreman went, came back and said, "Reg wants to see you in his office." Reg was the manager. He said, "I hear you want to leave. What's the trouble?" Norman explained everything and he said, "Tools cost money, haven't you got any?" (he meant the file he needed). Norman said, "I have all the tools I need to have. I'm not going to buy the tools you are supposed to provide. "Reg said, "There are broken drills and taps on the floor near your bench". Norman said, "If there is, I haven't put them there." Reg said, "You will have to serve a week's notice." Norman said, "I am not serving a weeks notice, I am finishing at 5.30pm.". he then went back to my bench. he still hadn't a job to do, so he sat on the bench. he had booked and paid for my dinner ticket in the canteen. Reg came in the work place and saw Norman sitting on the bench. He said, "Get off that bench, and get on with your work.". Norman said, "I haven't got any work and you are messing me about and I will mess you about now. I am not leaving at 5.30pm. he am leaving at Dinner time now."

Norman went for his dinner in the canteen, when the foreman came to him and said, "Reg wants you in his office he has your cards and money ready." he said, "He will have to wait, I am having my dinner." Norman finished his dinner and went to Reg's office. He had gone out for his. When he came back, he asked Norman to sign a paper saying that he wasn't entitled to any money in place of notice. he said, "I'll sign that when I've checked my pay and bonus." Norman checked everything and all was OK. So he collected his tools and bike. He checked my toolbox to see if he had anything belonging to the firm and he hadn't so off he went home.

When Norman got home Nancy said, "Why have you come home so early?". he explained what had happened. She was very worried and about that time Nancy was expecting their first child. They talked about having children, and thought they would like two boys and two girls and they agreed to both stop smoking, as it was better for the child.

One morning about 6am it was time to go for the midwife. Norman had to go on his bike about a mile to her house and knock her up. She was very slow. She had no bike, so they had to walk and Norman was very worried and thought the baby would be born before they got home. She wouldn't be rushed. They finally got there and the baby was born at 7.3Oam. 7lb 6 ounces, a girl, we called her Edith and all was well. Date 14/10/1946.

Football

Norman went to Manchester City Football Club for a trial to try and be a professional footballer. They took his name and he started training each evening. Norman had two games as an amateur playing full back, left or right. The manager was Sammy Cowan. City was in the second division. Sammy took them into the first division that year.

Training was at Manchester City Football Club Maine Road. Under the main Stand was an area where they used to learn to kick a football. The ball at that time, 1947 had a bladder in it, was leather and hard and very heavy when wet. They wore gym shoes, so if you kicked the ball wrongly it hurt your foot. The ground there was fine black cinder. There was a bit of a balcony where the coach used to stand and hang a football on a string. They had to line up and run after each other to try and head the ball, which was all over the place. They had to learn timing and that involved skipping like a boxer does, heel and toe and punching a pear shaped ball like a boxer does.

They was a ball with a spring attached to it, one spring going to the floor and one to the ceiling so that the ball was then head high. Norman was told to punch it then head it, the idea being to speed you up, in readiness for what you needed to do.

I punched the ball as hard as he could; it came back at me like a rocket and hit me in the face. That was a hard lesson to learn. So it was learn to control a ball, how to keep it low. How to be there before the ball gets to you when heading it. That's timing.

I had trouble with my left leg, varicose veins. So they said he couldn't play football with that leg, it was too risky. So he had to give up the idea.

CHAPTER 16

Next Jobs

Norman's next job was at T.C. Thompson. They were Printing engineers making printing machines. he was working with another fitter making the ink ducts for a Thompson Auto Platen. This was very much like the German Auto Platen, which his father had in his printing works. he was there for nine months till one day Norman was talking to another fitter near his bench, when the charge hand came up and said, "Break it up." he said, "Ok he won't be a minute." And because he didn't stop talking immediately, he stormed off and went to the under manager and came back and said, "You're on a weeks notice."

Norman had a day off the next day and he got a job at Dixon and Hawksworth in Middleton making circular saws for cutting trees up, after they had been chopped down. They also made cement mixers, both machines were on a frame making them portable and they were to be belt driven, by a tractor, or other drive units. One day Norman was having his lunch about 10am. When Dixon came into the shop he saw Norman on the bench eating his lunch. He got the foreman and pointed to Norman. The foreman came over and said, "Dixon said you are sacked for stopping work while eating." Norman said, "I can't eat and work at the same time, as my hands are very dirty. he had washed them for that reason." He said, "Sorry you are on a weeks notice." When he got home he told Nancy. She said, "It's you, you will never settle, there will be trouble where ever you go." he said, "I am not a robot and am not going to be used as one." he had only been there a week.

Norman then got a job at David Browns Machine Tools who made gear cutting machines. At that time they had a prefab on Heaton Park, Sheepsfoot Lane, off Middleton Road. It wasn't far to go to work on his bike to Browns. They only had a bed, a dining table, four chairs, a cot and pram and high chair, which folded down to a low chair. It had wheels, so Edith could push it, as she learnt to walk, from one end of the living room to the other. At the rear of their prefab was a fair size garden. And the railings of Heaton Park, which, part of, was used for a poor children's camp, for summer holidays. The rear of the garden was all silver sand which he didn't know at that time was good for lawns. As it was sloping towards the prefab, Norman dug a lot of it into the comer, and put wood round it to make a sand pit for Edith to play in when she was older. He also dug trenches to mix leaves, sand and soil, as the soil was wet and sticky near the prefab. It made the ground very good for growing veg. The job at Browns was very hard and Norman had a lot to learn. There were fine time limits, and skills to achieve. But it is what Norman needed to become a Skilled fitter so he settled in and was happy there. While Norman was there they started a football team and they went in to the Rusholme and District 1st Division. Most people thought they should have gone into a lower Division, being a new team. Their home ground was at Mellands playing fields, Mount Road, Gorton. Their first game was at home against Crossley Motors. They thought they were going to get hammered Norman was playing left full back. They kicked off, and very soon they were a goal down it took them a while to get settled in. Then they got their first goal, more were to follow and by halftime they were winning 4-1. They had a talk, and decided not to score too many goals, as other teams would be prepared for them. When the score got to7-1 they stopped scoring. The forwards would get the ball near their goals and instead of putting it in the net they would leave it and run away. During that time Edith was ill a lot, chicken pox, German measles, proper measles, scarlateena, whooping cough, which lasted six weeks. She was just at the stage of trying to walk. They were very worried; Norman thought they were going to lose her. The doctor said, "She is catching everything that is going about". He said, "If she had been breast fed these things wouldn't have happened. I think you had better leave this area for her sake." So they got another prefab (exchange) near Nancy's mothers in Moss-Side. Edith recovered there and was a lot better.

After a year and a half at Browns Sherbome Street, Norman was transferred to David Brown Jackson's in Salford, which David Browns had taken over. They had built a new big bay for large machines, which had been taken out of Germany. Two other fitters were transferred as well. The money the government owed David Browns for war work was part payment by these machines, which were dumped in fields and covered with tarpaulins. The rain got in some parts then froze so cracked the castings. The Germans who were stripping the machines sabotaged them. We found grease in oil pipes and when grease was removed they found sand inside. There were also steel rods driven between large roller bearings. So they had to strip & inspect everything.

It took nine months, with six fitters to install one machine. A German Waldritch, a vertical boring machine. The crosslide weighed 40 tons, two gearboxes with boring rams, which moved along with the crosslide, weighed nine tons each. Revolving table weighed 20 tons. You could go down steps and walk under the machine, to adjust the table bearings and set the balance mechanism for what weight you put on the table.

The football team's second match was away to Adelphi Lads Club, which they won 5-2. The team got a good write up, in the local paper. Their next match was at home, against Abbey Hey Workingmen's Club. They were winning 3-0, just before halftime the captain, who played centre half, passed back to the goal keeper by surprise, so ball went into the net. The captain gave the goalkeeper a mouthful. It was then halftime. A lot of players were arguing about it the goalkeeper was very upset, the team fell to pieces, so they then started to loose. They lost 6-3. After that the team broke up. He got made captain; they had lost most of their best players. So some games they won, some they lost. The next time, they played Abbey Hey on their ground.

Norman had to swap the team about, as they were players short. he noticed a young apprentice who followed the team about. He used to stand in the goals before the match started. He had big hands, so he thought he would make a good goalkeeper. he took the goalkeeper they were using. Not the one they used to have, and put him in my place, left fullback. he put the young lad in goal. he put the rest of the team in the places they said they could play in. he had to play inside left. he had a young lad 15 years of age, at outside left, another at outside right. he told them both to stay up, but watch the offside. he told the young lad on my left to watch for me putting the ball on the inside of the fullback and for him to then cut in and go for goal. He did that and scored the first goal. The one on the right did the same, so they were winning 2-0. Norman had the ball in his own half and a player was on him and he couldn't shake him off. So he belted the ball towards their goal. It went into the goal, top right hand corner. A real (Beckham) goal. They got one back, so the score was 3-1 for them. They got a penalty, the young lad saved it. All the people watching came to their goals, to see the young goalkeeper. He was tipping the ball round the post over the bar. They couldn't score. They said, "Where have you got him from? You won't have him long, all the big clubs will be after him."

So they got their own back for the match they lost 6-3.

After a year and a half at David Brown Jackson's, the job finished, so Norman was moved to the foundry. he was there a week and didn't like it. So he left and got a job at Gresham and Cravens. he had been at David Browns three years and learned a lot. Gresham's was near Browns also in Salford.

The job he had at Gresham's was reconditioning machines, Norman worked in the maintenance department. he was the only fitter doing reconditioning as the others were on general maintenance. The first machine he recondition was a Darling and Sellers Centre Lathe seven ft long bed. Norman stripped it down, then he looked for a bridge strip to check the bed for wear. he asked the charge hand where the bridge strip and surface plates were. He said, "Bridge strip, what's that?" he told him what it was, and that he needed at least a six ft one, and a 14" square surface plate. He went to see the foreman in the tool room, who came to see me. He said, "What do you want these things for?" he told him. He said "These things cost a lot of money, other fitters have done the machines before and they didn't want the things you are asking for." he said, "They may have cleaned, polished and painted them to look nice, but no way had they reconditioned them without the things he have asked for." He then said, "We have a 3ft straight-edge." he said, "three ft in seven ft is no used at all." He said, "Ok we will get them." he found out the tool room foreman used to be the chauffeur for the boss and was not an engineer at all. The men in the tool room ran the place and the maintenance charge hand was a semi-skilled capstan operator. When he got the bridge strip and put it on the bed. He found the bed was worn .035 in the middle, so needed planing. he told the foreman it needed planing. He said, "We haven't a planer big enough to take that bed." he said, "You will have to send it out then, David Browns can do it." He said, "You will have to file it and scrape it by hand." he said, "It will take months to do it that way." He wouldn't pay to have it done, so it took Norman months to do it by hand. The bed was 5" wide on one side, 4" on the other side. Two 90 degrees in the centre, and 45 degrees on each outer sides. So he had to make a set of trammel blocks to do it with.

Nancy's mother didn't live far away, so he could go to work, and she would look after Nancy and Edith. Norman had a hard job doing the lathe, which took me five months, as they knew nothing about reconditioning. So he had to run the job himself completely. When finished, it was installed, tested and started producing parts. The next machine was a German Automatic. He worked on it for two months; it needed a lot of new parts. Norman got fed up with the foreman and charge hand. Told them they knew nothing about Engineering. So he started to look for another job and it took him a few months before he found one suitable.

CHAPTER 17

New Son. New Job. New Dog

Nancy was pregnant with their second child. One Saturday night, Norman went to the British Legion which was near by, with a brother-in-law for a drink. he left Nancy with her Mother and sister, May to look after her and Edith. On returning home about 10.30pm, As he knocked on the prefab door, and May opened it he heard a baby crying. The midwife and doctor was there and the midwife only lived in the street opposite and after a while when Norman could see the baby and Nancy, he looked at the baby, which looked about three months old. Was 10. 3/41bs. It had a big broad nose and thick lips like a darkie. he said, "It's a good Job he is white." So gave Nancy a big hug and kiss. We had a lovely son.

One day Norman didn't go to work and went looking for a job. There was nothing much good at the employment office. So he went to the union head office up town A.E.U. They gave him a card to go to Massey-Harris Ltd, a firm that made farm machinery. The job was in the Maintenance department. It was in Trafford Park an industrial area. he went there and got the job. So next day he went to Gresham's and gave his notice in. Started at Massey's on Monday. The foreman put him with another fitter, to show him the way around the place. He was the overtime champion of the maintenance department. So he was working overtime right away, weekdays as well as weekends. Norman had go to work on a bike so it was hard going, working all those hours. The bloke he worked with had a car, so it was okay for him. Still the money was good, so they could buy things they couldn't have before. The war started in Korea, after he had been at Massey's about four months, Norman was doing his turn of nights, (One fitter to look after the full factory). They did two weeks a turn. Norman was on reserve with the Royal Navy. Norman received his calling up papers to go, while he was on nights.

He took his papers in to show the foreman the next morning, before going home. He looked at them and said, "I will have to show them to the maintenance engineer." He phoned him, who came to see Norman. He said, "I can't have you going away. We will have to get you off this." He tried to get him off it, but to no avail. Norman had to go to HMS DRAKE Barracks, Keyham, Devonport. he didn't have to go for three months. So he had time to prepare for it.

Norman went to the dogs home Harpurhey. he had to get two buses to get there, one from Moss-Side to town, then one from the bus station to Harpurhey. he looked at the dogs in a large compound. Found a black and white sheep dog, a border collie. It was nervous.

Norman paid seven and sixpence for it. They gave him some rope to tie round it's neck. It looked At him with a sad look. he gave it a pat and a stroke to make it feel wanted. Then off they went to the bus stop. It was a double decker bus, and the dog wasn't allowed on the lower deck. So had to take it on to the top deck. It wouldn't go up the stairs, so he had to carry it up. When he got home to the prefab, Nancy and Edith liked the dog. Made a fuss of it, gave it a drink and something to eat. They then got a large cardboard box for it to sleep in. After a while it settled down.

When they had it for a week, he gave it a wash in the bath, it didn't like it at first, he had to hold it by the collar, and it shook its self and made a right mess in the bathroom. After he dried it, then combed and brushed it. he took it for a walk in the Park. It was walking along feeling very proud and happy with its nice clean coat. It soon took to Norman, and was very easy to train. He could get it to walk along side of him without the lead. They kept it in the back garden for a while, till it settled in and got used to them and they called it Shep. Then it used to sit at the front door path. If anyone came near it would growl.

So they had to keep it in the house or back garden. When Norman got home from work on his bike, it would Jump the gate and stop him, he had to get it off; it was very pleased to see him.

CHAPTER 18

Back In The Navy. H.M.S. Howe

The time came for Norman to go to Pymouth, H.M.S. Drake Barracks, in Keyham Devonport. When he arrived there he had a medical, sorted out his kit and mess. Then next day he had to go to the Gunnery School to brush up on the up- to- date guns and ordnance work. This took about two weeks. Then he was given a long weekend leave. Before he was to be drafted on to H.M.S. Howe battleship with 14" Guns. When he got home everyone was surprised to see him home so soon. The dog went mad jumping up at him, and followed him about. Nancy and the children were happy to see him. Nancy said, the dog was howling all night when Norman went away, looking all over for him. Norman's son then was about eight months old, Edith about four years old. He had a good weekend then went back to join the Battleship H.M.S. Howe. It was tied up at the jetty. Part of the Moth Ball Fleet. The guns were covered with netting and plastic covering. he had to report to the Ordnance Officer.

After he had settled in to mess on the first day, he was to work with Ordnance Artificers.

On the first Sunday on H.M.S. Howe. They had church parade, so had to fall in on the top deck. Wearing number ones uniform and wearing their medals. A Rear Admiral came to inspect them. He could tell the reserves to by the medals they were wearing.

He stopped and spoke to some as he walked along the ranks. When he came to Norman. He asked him how he liked being back. he said, "I don't", He said, and "how is that? he said, "I have a wife and two children to support. I had a good Job in Civvy Street, with good wages, what I will get here is peanuts compared with it and I expected to get called up when there is a war on, not this Korea matter; you have enough ships to put a blockade on Korea without calling the reserves up. I was doing more important work in Civvy Street than what I will be doing here". He said," What were you doing in Civvy Street?" Norman said, "As you will know the number one priority is mechanization of the farms, to grow food better and quicker, as people are still on rations. I was working at a firm that made farm machinery". He said, "You will be doing important work here". And walks on.

One day the Ordnance Officer asked Norman if he could work a lathe, he said, "yes", He said he wanted a standard lamp making, it would have to be in four parts, so that he could put it in a suitcase. The base, the column was to be in three parts with a hole down the centre for the electric wire and it would have to have a metal tube to join each part together. Norman made it, it had to be bees waxed, rubbed into the wood. The Officer was delighted with it. Then he wanted another one made for his pal. So Norman did that also.

Norman had to go into the Royal Navy Hospital in Stonehouse Plymouth. For an operation on his left leg, for varicose veins. After the opp, they said you can play football again now.

Norman played football every Thursday afternoon for the Ordnance Artificers. One day he was asked if he would like to play for the Reserve Fleet. he said, "I don't mind". They said," you will play every Wednesday afternoon". In the Forces 1 't Division against Army, Navy and Air force teams. The first game he played was against the Coastal Artillery. He had to meet the teams outside the Dockyard Gate (Albert Gate). When he got there he found they were a man short, he was a sick bay attendant, who had to take a sick man to Hospital. He played Outside Left.

They were playing away at the Army Barracks, a coach was to take them there. The team consisted of players from different ships, four from the Howe, so they kicked off with ten men, very soon they were a goal down, the right half handed the ball. A penalty, they scored. It took the team about 20 minutes to settle down. Then they started to play and they soon scored, and kept scoring. They won 7-1. It was like that every game, They won them all. They played the Royal Engineering College with ten men, won 6-2. They were top of the League. The Royal Marines were second, they beat them 2-1.

H.M.S. Drake. Barracks was third. They won every game, was in the semi-final of the cup. They would have won both but the team broke up as players got drafted.

Norman was drafted onto a destroyer H.M.S. Alamein a battle class which was to be towed by a large sea going tug to Liverpool. Other work he did while on the Howe involved the secondary armament; the 5.25 Guns, three twin gun turrets making six guns each side of the ship, towards the rear near the bridge which made 12 guns in all. Norman worked on them on his own, making parts on a lathe and he did six guns before going on the destroyer.

One day on shore leave from the Howe, Norman was on the last liberty boat 11pm. He was halfway there and was having a cig when a Petty Officer, shouted, "Put that cigarette out". He shouted, "shut your mouth up, you are not on duty, you are on shore leave the same as me, so shut it". When Norman got back on board, onto the quarter deck the Petty Officer was waiting for him, with the Officer of the watch.

He told him that Norman was smoking and when told to put it out, he refused. The officer told Norman that he would be on commanders report. It was a few days before Norman saw the

Commander. When he saw him as a defaulter and Norman stood before him. The Regulating Petty Officer shouts. "Attention, off cap". The Commander read the charge out, which was "smoking in unlawful places, on the liberty boat at 11pm". He said to Norman, "what have you got to say for yourself?" Norman said. "I admit I was smoking Sir, but it was dark, I didn't know it was the Petty Officer here that was speaking. I thought it was one of my mates, skylarking". He said, to the Petty Officer," what have you got to say about that?" He said," it was not dark, there was a light shining from the wheel house.", He asked Norman what he had to say about that?, Norman said, "there is no light shining from the wheel house when the vessel is under way, if there was a man on the wheel he wouldn't be able to see where he was going". The Commander gave the Petty Officer a right look. Then he turned to Norman and said, "For smoking in unlawful places, seven days No.11 punishment." The Regulating Petty officer, shouted, "seven days No.11 punishment on cap, left turn, double march".

Norman then had to go to the Master at Arms Office to find out when and where he would start his punishment.

There were twenty punishments in the Royal Navy. No 11, the one used mostly, was shore leave stopped, do work in your free time and be called out anytime during the night.

You had to hang a notice on your hammock with your name on it and put your name on your hammock, in the quarter masters day book, on the quarter deck every day. So you could be found at any time during the night if needed. Also listen to loudspeakers at all times for, "Men under Punishment to Muster", it would then say where to go.

During free time in the evening the men had to fall in on the upper deck for one hours drill. There was always a few late for drill and then had another day added on.

A Petty Officer took the drill, which was with a rifle; you ran round in a circle, holding the rifle with both hands above your head, it became heavy, so it touched your head, so you started to shuffle. He shouted get your knees up up up, so the rifle was banging on your head, after a while he changes it, "Slope arms," The rifle was then resting on your collar bone which wears the skin off. He then changes it to the other side and wears the skin off that collar bone.

He changes to different drill positions each to make your arms ache. After the hour you went to the sick bay to get a dressing on your collar bones. You still had to do it next day and for how many Days you have got punishment. Other Punishments are pay stopped.

CHAPTER 19

Destroyer H.M.S Alamein

Norman was going onto the destroyer H.M.S. Alamein because it was a compassionate draft to Liverpool, as my wife Nancy had been attacked in Moss Side, Manchester and was not able to stay in the prefab, she had to go home to her mother with the two children. That would mean he would lose his home. The ordnance officer arranged it for Norman. He boarded the destroyer in Plymouth; there was only a small crew about 12. It was a towing job and there was no main engine, only the secondary one to drive the generator, to give them electricity and it was in need of repair. A large sea going tug was to tow them to Liverpool. It was estimated to take three days. They had to have two black balls up the mast to show, a vessel underway, but not under command. At night time two white lights were up the mast for same signal and the port and starboard lights as well as bow and stem lights.

They set sail on a Monday morning in January, 1951. Weather cold and windy. They were on a short tow first, until they got into the open sea on the English Channel off Plymouth, it was a few miles and the weather worse. By the time they got off the Bristol Channel They were in a storm, which lasted 18 hours. During the storm they could hear on the radio about a liberty ship in the same storm. It broke in half; a man swam with a line from one half to the other half.

When he heard that on the radio, he thought we would have fired a line by a gun, then a rope tied to it, then a wire hawser and then they would winch the two halves together. That's what they did and the man was called Dante, an American ship was called The Flying Enterprise.

The storm was very bad so the tug stopped towing, the sea was coming in, and the mess deck was a foot deep in sea water. The secondary engine packed in. So there were neither lights up the mast at night nor steaming lights, or lights below deck there was no electricity for cooking. They had to use paraffin lamps for up the mast they would haul them up and the wind would blow them out, then we would take them in the wheelhouse and light them again, this kept happening," what a carry on," and it was also pouring with rain. For their meals they had to use primas stoves, tie the pans to them, and then tie the lot to the hammock bars. They kept their clothes on all the time, as all was wet and damp, hammocks included. The voyage took five days not three, so we had to ration food.

When they arrived in Liverpool, they couldn't go up the Mersey weather too bad. They were stuck outside port for another 18 hours. They got alongside Princess Landing Stage at 7pm on the Friday night. The Captain was waiting for them; He had come up to Liverpool by train. He was a Lieutenant Commander. The last time Norman saw him, he was on the Rodney as a leading seaman, called Slinger Wood. He told them all to go home till Monday morning. One of the sailors was very ill with rheumatic fever. The L.C. said, "He needs hospital near his home in Manchester, to save his wife coming to visit him in Liverpool." So two of them who lived in Manchester took him home. They were all not feeling so good. Norman had Bronchitis; he couldn't go sick as that might have meant him being sent back to Plymouth. Norman had to get himself better which took a long time.

They couldn't live on the ship. So unless your home was in Liverpool, you had to find digs. Norman had relatives in Birkenhead, so he went to see them, to ask could he put down that he was staying there. As he wanted to go home every night to Manchester. Norman would get money from the Navy for lodging allowance. They said they would agree to it. They were pleased to see him and they had a good chat and some food and drink.

On the Friday night after seeing the sick shipmate home, who lived in Wythenshawe, Norman went home a few miles away from his friend, he lived in a prefab in Moss Side, The first thing he noticed was no dog. Norman said to Nancy, "where is the dog?" Nancy said," it went mad after you went back to join H.M.S. Howe. So we had to have it put down, it was going for us all and it was looking all over the place for you." Norman felt very upset as he had got used to that dog. Still he had a good weekend. Norman had to get up early Monday morning 5am to catch the 6am train at Manchester Central Station, which is now called G-Mex an Exhibition for Liverpool and had to be on board the destroyer H.M.S Alamein by 8am. Norman used to book a workman's ticket to Warrington, stay on the train and pay the excess fare, When he got to Liverpool, the train was a non corridor type one, so had no toilets and was cold. When he got to the ship, that was cold, being a dead-ship.

Norman was working with a second class Artificer on the guns. He also had to go to Cammell Lairds for the mail every morning. The ship had to go into dry dock.

One day after being in the dry dock a few weeks. They were being moved to the other side of the Mersey to Birkenhead, a tug or two was to do the job, they had to catch the tide early at 6am and as he couldn't go home the day before. He slept on board in a cabin, another shipmate did the same. As they were coming out of the basin to enter the river, a gust of wind blew them against the corner of the entrance to the basin and put a big dent in the ships side. They had to go back into dry dock again.

All the wires, ropes and flags were being renewed and the Artificer and Norman were doing a lot of work on the guns, seals, some modifications too.

The ship had a big refit, took eight months. Then it was time to go back to Plymouth for demob again. Just before that Norman was trying to get another home away from the prefab. He was at the Council Housing Offices every Saturday morning Norman finally got a three bedroom house in Wythenshawe. The Captain gave him three weeks leave to move into it. Then he went back to Plymouth and H.M.S Drake barracks for demob.

When the war was over and Norman was waiting for demob in the barracks at H.M.S. Drake.

Devonport. Plymouth. Norman used to spend some time in the canteen, where you could have a pint of beer and something to eat and there were plenty of matlos (slang for sailor,)

Who would entertain them with stories, tricks and songs. Young sailors start at age 15 to 18 that is Boy's Service which doesn't count as Service. Then from 18 to 20 is classed as under age.

You were not allowed rum till you were 20. You were then a man.

SONG

"Come gather round you sailor boys and listen to
my plea. When you hear my story, pity me.
For I was a goddam fool, in the port of Liverpool,
the first time that I came home from sea.
We were paid off at the Hoe, from a ship called Sierra
Leone, four pound ten a month was all my pay.

And drinking rum and gin, I was very soon taken in
by a little girl whose name was Maggie May. Oh well
do I remember, the time I met Maggie May.
She was cruising up and down Old Cannon Place.
She wore a dress so fine, her figure was divine,
and so me being a matlo, I gave chase.
Next morning I awoke, my clothes there I to find,
but no trousers, silk or lanyard could I find.
When I asked her where they were, she said, my dear kind
Sir, they're down at Paddy's pawn shop, number nine.
To the pawn shop I did go, just my hat and coat, you
know, but no trousers, silk or Lanyard did I find.

So a policeman came and took that girl away.
The judge he guilty found her, for robbing a homeward
bounder, and paid her passage back to
Botany Bay.
Oh Maggie Maggie May they have taken her
away, down Old Cannon Place.
She will Cruise no more. For she had robbed many a poor Sailor,
The Captain of the whaler, now she is doing time in Botany Bay.

CHAPTER 20

Back In Civvy Street Again

It had been 18 months. Norman was back home and he got his job back at Massey Harris. It was October 1952 and he soon settled into his job again working overtime and weekends, as the firm was very busy, mechanization of the farms was number one priority As he was in the maintenance dept he sometimes worked late to finish work on a breakdown.

After Norman had been back six months he started to play football again; he played for a team called Duro Sports, in South Manchester Wythenshawe League, Started at left fullback, after a few months, he was made captain and moved to centre half. They had different players taking a penalties Norman won it. So every time they won a penalty he took it and he never missed.

One day he had two in the first half and scored. In the second half, they got one.

Norman had a relative who had been a professional footballer and he told me to try a bit of Psychology and this day Norman tried it. As soon as they had the penalty awarded against them, Norman went to their goal keeper and told him he was just trying to put this man off his shot, he waved Norman's arms about to make it look as if he was instructing the keeper what to do.

Norman then started to walk out of the penalty area, as he was doing that, the man who was about to take the kick, said, "What have you told him? Where you are going to put it?" Norman said,

"You will be surprised where you will put it."

He put it right over the crossbar and hee looked at me with astonishment.

When two of Norman's team mates saw him walking to the goalkeeper, they thought he was going to pace the penalty spot out, as it was the same spot he had used in the first half, They shouted, "Come off it", he had not told anyone what he was going to do.

The goal keeper only knew when he told him. He never used that trick again, as Norman liked to win by fair play.

CHAPTER 21

Turkey Gets The Axe

Life was very hard for Norman working overtime and weekends, but they needed the money to get back on their feet, after low pay in the Navy. Christmas came and Nancy won a turkey at the local butchers. It was too big to go in the oven. So Norman said," We will have to cut it in two, he got the axe and gave it a mighty blow, forgetting about the stuffing inside, which went all over the kitchen. Nancy was in tears, about the mess and the poor turkey. So he cleared up the mess and started to do surgery on the turkey. He made it into two birds and stitched up with stuffing inside. They cooked them both. They had a good Christmas considering, the trouble was they had too much turkey and they couldn't give it away. They were sick of turkey, Norman was taking it for his lunch to work for two weeks. After riding a bike to work at Trafford Park for six miles Norman got a motorbike. It was only a 98cc two stroke, two speed and he bought it new from Kings the motorbike people. Norman soon found it was faulty on the gear change. So he took it back, they tried it, said, "there's nothing wrong with it." So he sorted it out himself and he found the index plate for the gear lever had been made wrong.

It was a hardened plate, he had to grind 1/16 of an inch, off the low position. It then was OK. It was no use for Norman to pass his test on, as if he was behind a car with a four speed gearbox, his first gear was too high to go slow, it would stall, if he didn't slip the clutch. So he failed his test twice with it. Norman then got a 197cc Bike with a three speed gearbox, passed his test first time with it.

During that time Nancy was pregnant again with our third child.

She complained about her left leg calf muscle and they said it was the weight she was carrying and it would be OK after the baby was born. As she was having the baby at home. Edith and Leslie went to stay with their Aunty May. he was at work when the baby was born, had the day off before, but it was a false alarm. The midwife came with a young nurse and went away thinking Nancy wasn't ready, but left the young nurse and while she was away Nancy started. It was the first time for the nurse, and the cord was round the baby's neck. Nancy had to help her and tell her what to do. They managed OK, by the time the midwife came back, all was over. They phoned Norman at work to say a baby girl had been born and he went home right away. Nancy asked the nurse what her name was, she said "Margaret". Nancy told her, she would name the baby after her "Margaret"; she was very pleased about that. Norman phoned work to say he was having a week off. After the baby was three days old, Nancy was still complaining about her calf muscle, so he got some Algipan and rubbed her leg with it. She then became very ill and was coughing blood up. So Norman dialled 999, ambulance came and took them all to Nell Lane hospital. After a short while a doctor came to Norman, he was very angry, told him, "never to massage anything without knowing what you are doing." Nancy had a clot of blood in her leg, which Norman had broken up, so it went to her lung, it could have gone to her heart or brain and killed her. Nancy was in hospital for about two weeks. Edith & Leslie went to school in Moss Side during that time.

Norman had trouble with the two stroke motorbike. The 98cc one, after he had it nine months, it was bad starting. he tried everything, everything was set right. he had to run with it, to get it started. One day he was running with it, and it started suddenly, he fell on his knees, but still had hold of the handlebars, which caused him to work the twist grip (throttle) and increase the speed, so he was dragged along on his knees for about 10 or 12 yards.

But Norman couldn't let go, thinking the bike would fall on him, so he steered the front wheel into the kerb, to stop it, he then worked the clutch lever to disengage the power. The engine was still going, so he got on the bike and went to work. When he got there, he looked at his knees, overalls and trousers had a big hole in them. Norman's knees were badly torn to the bone. So he went to the nurse at work, who put dressings on and bandaged them up.

Norman found out that the fuel needed to have the flash point raised. he did that by putting some neat petrol in the tank. From then on he put less oil in the petrol tank. The 197cc was a lot better. The only trouble he had with that was, the lead in the petrol caused a whisker to bridge the gap in the spark plug from time to time, so caused the engine to stop. He had to take the spark plug out, cut the whisker away, put plug back and away again.

At that time all the departments bar the maintenance departments at Massey — Harris Ltd, were getting wage increases. Norman went to see the convenor (head union man) Norman said, "I am fed up with your department, not having a shop steward," "you take it on." he said, "I am new here and I don't know my way around enough yet." So after a few months, Norman took the stewards job on.

Norman put in for a wage increase for all the maintenance department. Asked for a reply in a week and he got it, so all the maintenance got a rise.

Things went well from then on. Norman's father in law George Pitts was like a father to him and his mother in law Ninny Pitts (Mary) was like a mother. George Pitts worked for the G.P.O. as a driver on parcel post. He took Norman to buy a van at Quick's Motors, Old Trafford. It was a 10 C.W.T. Ford 11 HP, with a three speed gear box, crash gears. He taught Norman to drive it and he passed his test first time.

At first he kept it in the Grove where he lived in Wythenshawe. Then he kept it in a farm near by.

The farmer wouldn't let him work on it. So one day a neighbour said he would swap houses with Norman who lived at 23. Longcroft Grove, his neighbour lived at no 4 where there was room to have a Garage where as Norman's just had a pathway. So they swapped houses. Norman got a chance to buy the Council House and he bought it.

Norman put a garage up and put three windows in each side of the van. He took the rear doors off and made new doors to open up and down. He put in a three seater at the back and a two seater in the middle and two seats at the front making it a seven seater family car.

Edith was now seven. She asked could she have music lessons, to play the piano. Nancy and Norman had a talk about it, so they said, "Yes", she could have music lessons and he would get a Piano for her. he bought a second hand one and had it tuned.

She went to lessons and did an hours practice every day, was very keen to learn.

When they moved to 4 Longcroft, Norman made a two wheel trolley to move the piano on and it did the job a treat.

As time went on she had a new teacher, he had a band, and lived nearby and he came to their house to teach her.

A few years went by. A new fitter started at Massey's. The foreman put him with Norman and showed him the ropes. He was 20years older than Norman. They got on OK. He also could play the piano, but couldn't read music. He could play any type of music and he was like a concert pianist. He came to their house and got on the piano with Edith they were a duet. Edith was playing and reading music, he fitted in perfect and it was wonderful.

About that time the balers which picked up the hay in the farms and tie it up, then drop it off as it went along being towed by a tractor, started to have faults on them and all had to be returned to the factory. First they had insects on them and workers were getting bitten. The balers had to be steam cleaned, before they went into the factory. There was balers everywhere even on the sports field and football pitches at the end of the factory and everyone was very busy.

The school for the children was very near it was both infants and juniors. One day when Nancy was getting the children ready for bed, she noticed Leslie had some bruises on his back. She asked him how he had got them, he didn't want to tell her, she insisted, so he said," it was the teacher."

Norman was on night work at the time. The next morning before going to bed, he went to see the Headmaster. He sent for Leslie and the Deputy Head, who was the one who was involved in looking after the children at playtime. When he arrived. He said, "when I blew the whistle for the children to fall in and line up, before going back into the classrooms, Leslie was playing about and not getting in line, So I gave him a few smacks." Norman said, "send Leslie back to his class, I don't want him to hear what I have to say to you." So Leslie went away. Norman said to the Headmaster, "When you are dealing with children you have to use a bit of discretion, not manhandle them." He said, "The Deputy Head has not got where he is today by not having any discretion, are you against corporal punishment?" Norman said, "I don't mollycoddle my children, I am firm and strict with them. But I am not going to allow anyone to knock them about. If they do wrong, send them home with a letter, you will know I have received it, as I will send you a reply." "Give them lines to do. I will see they do them. If there is any more of this going on and I have to come here again. I won't be talking to you nice and you will see the other side of me. I am on night work, should be in bed now and not talking to you, good morning," Norman then went home.

CHAPTER 22

Spirit Leaves Then Comes

While still at 23, Longcroft and Norman was about 32 years of age and he had to have a hernia operation on his right side. This was done at Nell Lane hospital. It was in the summer months and all was well, it was Wednesday and he was going back to work on the following Monday. Norman started to feel ill, so he went to bed. Nancy sent for the doctor. He said, "You have got pneumonia." He was coming twice a day giving Norman injections and he felt very weak and very ill. After about a week or less, he knew he was dying, till about 4am one morning. He felt something leave his body from between his ribs at the lower part, called, solar plexus. he didn't know what it was at that time and after a short time he felt the same, something return to his body. When the doctor came in the morning at 11 am. He said," How are you this morning?" Norman said, "I am starting to feel better," the doctor then told him what had happened at 4am. He said, "You have gone through the crisis, if you hadn't got through that, you would have been dead. That was your spirit leaving you and coming back. You had delayed shock, which caused pneumonia. When a person has an operation the nervous system suffers a shock, it usually happens while on the table, so doctors and surgeons can deal with it. You didn't have it then, you had delayed shock and that's what caused the pneumonia. You will be all right now and get better." So after another week or so, Norman went back to work. he was using Edith's bed, in the back bedroom, she slept with her mum. Leslie was in the box room. Edith was eight, Leslie was four. Life was very hectic with all the hours he was working, playing football, doing the garden and jobs in the house. As time went on, he had plenty of cases as a shop steward to deal with. One was a strike at the weekend. The firm got contractors in without consulting Norman. First the electricians, found outsiders working on the electric stoves in the canteen, he went to see the outriders and asked them for their union card, they had none. Then they found there were plumbers on the factory. Their workmen had been laid off. Norman went to see the foeman. The maintenance men were ready to stop work and walk out. When he found the foreman, he said he would phone the managing director, who came to the factory. he went into the office with him. He said," what is the trouble." Norman said," Outside workmen have been brought into this factory, without consultation our maintenance men have been laid off, when they can do the job. It is an agreement that this does not happen, without consulting the shop stewards first."

CHAPTER 23

Promoted To Charge Hand

He fully agreed with Norman. He said, "seeing they are here, will you agree to let them carry on this once, I will reprimand the maintenance engineer who has done this and it will be brought up at the next works committee meeting and put in the minutes which you always attend and kept as a record and signed by all." I said, "I will now talk to the men and tell them what you have said and ask them to agree". Norman did that and they agreed and all was peaceful.

Norman did a lot of work on the van, painted it and used it for going to work. One day he was giving a labourer a lift home from work, as he turned right, he lent on the van door handle, so the door flew open and he was going out, Norman grabbed him by the coat and pulled him back in, saying, "we are not there yet." There was a catch near the handle to stop that happening, so he made sure people put that on, after that as time went on. The works manager called Norman in the office along with one of the electricians. He said, "I am offering you two the charge hands jobs. You will be supervisory, not working charge hands and the reason is the foreman will be retiring in 18 month time. One of you will take his place" "You will take his place Moors." "not you" He said to the electrician. "You will both work fortnights about nights and days, you will also get an increase in wages, starting next month. That will give you time to think about it." Norman went home that day and told Nancy, she was pleased about it, but was not sure about the nights work. he was doing six weeks days and two weeks nights at that time. So he said he will give it a try. Norman talked to his father in law about it, he said, "See how it goes." about that time, one of the fitters, said his son had a motor bike in bits and couldn't put it together again. Would Norman buy it from him. he said, "I will come and see it one night in my van," he went, it was an old one, A 1939 250cc OHV B.S.A. Girder Forks, Rigid Rear. He said, "parts may be missing and he may not be able to get spares for it. I'll take a chance." he gave him £5, he said, "OK". So he put it in the van and went home.

When he started work on it, he stripped it more, frame as well, he rebuilt it completely. That took him about a year. The working nights and day's fortnights about didn't give him much time for anything and Nancy didn't like being on her own at night a lot. The children didn't like it as they had to be quiet when Norman was in bed during the day and didn't get much sleep.

CHAPTER 24

Accidents On Motorbikes

One night Norman was going to work on his motorbike, he had to be there before 8pm for the start of the night shift. It was winter and the road was icy, he was on Brooklands Road and had to turn left at Brooklands Station on the Marsland Road, he changed to first gear, turned left on to the road bridge and started to go down the road which had the camber of the road the wrong way. he had made a wide turn because of the ice and he was in the middle of the road, he felt the bike sliding, a car was coming up the road towards him and he was going to go under the car, so he flung the bike down and to the left, he finished up with the bike lying on both my legs, facing towards the top of the hill, he was on a bus route, so if he didn't get out of the way quickly, he would have been run over and he struggled to get the bike off his legs. he couldn't get free. A man ran over to him and lifted the back wheel up. So he got his legs free and got up and got the bike to the side of the road. he thanked the man very much. Then Norman looked at his right leg which had had the brake lever stuck in it and above his knee on the right side. The handle bars were bent and the foot rest. Norman had to get to work to start the plant up. So it was a bit difficult to ride, but he made it to Massey's. Norman went to the nurse again, started the plant up first then later repaired the bike. Norman used the van then, until he sold the bike and rebuilt the B.S.A.250cc one. Norman had plenty to do until that day came. Nancy only went on the back of the motorbike once and she was too tense and affected the steering. Edith went on the back many times and she was OK.

Norman used to take Edith to his sister Dora, who lived in a cottage in Arley, Cheshire. They had a caravan which they towed when on holiday and Edith went with them. They had a boy who they had adopted and he was called Bryan and he was younger than Edith.

Norman had two accidents on the B.S.A. motorbike, one while he was working at Massey's. he was on nights at that time. he was on his way to work and he had to be there before 8pm, to start the plant up. he was on Marsland Road, stopped at the traffic lights, waiting to go right; there was a car in front of him and he wasn't signalling, but the position he was in. Norman was expecting him to be turning right as well. Marsland Road was a wide road, the road opposite was a narrow one and was on a bend just before the lights. The road he was going to turn on to was a main road, Chester Road. The lights changed to green, so car in front moved forward, so did Norman, then the car in front suddenly moved to the left, as well as going forward. he was in first gear and had his right hand out to show he was going to turn right, a car from the road opposite then hit him head on, he heard a big bang, was looking at legs in the air, they were Norman's, he was coming down upside down and he landed on his left shoulder, on the car bonnet, his crash helmet against the car windscreen. he then fell off onto the road, as the car stopped. The man (driver) opened the car door, his face white as a ghost; he thought he had killed Norman. He said," are you alright?" Norman said," I don't know yet, I can't feel anything." It was pouring with rain. He had P.V.C. over trousers on and Wellington boots. There was a big tear in the over trousers. he felt his leg wet, thought it was rain getting in where the tear was. A woman said, "I live just near, you can put your bike in my front garden and have a cup of tea, you must be in shock", he said, "Thank you, but let me get my senses together for a while first, Norman needed to think."

He told the driver he was going to the police station to report this accident and he had better come with him. He agreed, put his bike in the woman's garden, and then went to the police station. he asked the police to phone his firm up for him. As he wouldn't be going to work that night. They did that and then they both had to fill in a report form.

The driver of the car lived near Norman, so he gave him a lift home. It was about 11 pm when he got home. he knocked on the door to get Nancy up. She looked out of the bedroom window and said, "What are you doing coming home at this time for?" he said, "open the door and I'll tell you all about it". They went into the kitchen and he told her he has had an accident. he then started to take his wellington boots off, the left one first. Norman found the tear in the over trousers was not letting rain in, his boot was full of blood. So off he went to Wythenshawe hospital. Norman's leg was swollen and had a big cut in it and it had to be stitched up. So Norman had a week off work. Then he got the bike back in the van. It was badly damaged. forks bent, front wheel bent, so he put it in the garage till later much later.

CHAPTER 25

Leave Massey's For A.E.I.

Norman then made his mind up to leave Massey's and get a regular day job. So he went to the A.E. I. (The big House). He got a job there, and had to go back the following day, to find out where he would be working. he went into the personal department and was told," Sorry we have no job for you," he was very angry. he said, "what is going on? Yesterday he had a job, today you say he hasn't" Then Norman said," my brother works here." They said, "Does he? Who is your brother?" He said, "George Moors." They said, "wait a minute, "went out of the room and came back 15minutes later, he gave Norman an envelope with Mr Harrison written on it. They said," take this to Mr Harrison, go out of here, turn right, you will come to some large doors with a small door in them, go in there, that is B aisle, there are very large machines in there, walk down the middle pathway till you get to the end, go out turn left; first left go in there that is the Millwrights Dept". he made his way to the Millwrights Department, as instructed. he gave the letter to Mr Harrison. He read it and then said, "When can you start?" Norman said, "next Monday". He said," You will be working in this department, if you have tools and a car you can drive it into here you will have a bench with a large drawer and cupboard in it for your tools.

So off he went home and told Nancy he had got a new job and there would be no nights working from now on. Nancy and the children were delighted. Norman went back next day to Massy's to give his notice in. They wanted to know why, after being there eleven years. Norman said," it is the night work, which is upsetting my family. I have got a regular day job". The manager said," If you could have stuck it for another year, you would have been foreman and on regular days." Norman said, "a year is too long to expect my family to put up with the upset. Sorry but my plans have now been made", he shook his hand, and then walked out of his office.

Norman started at the A.E.I. one Monday morning, and drove the van into the Millwrights Department.

Mr Harrison the Foreman showed Norman his bench, so he put all his tools and gear in it. Then he drove the van to the car park and came back and he put Norman with another fitter, Charlie Wood, he also had been in the Navy. Norman showed him around the factory, and he was assigned to work with him on the job he was on. Installing a large lathe, they got on great. The machines were the largest in the world over 200ton. They were called Mammoth Machines. The shafts to be turned in the lathes weighed 80x90 ton. They were for the steam turbines for power stations. Norman was with Charlie for three months. Then he had jobs of his own and he had a fitters mate with him at all times, some were OK some were not and he finally got a regular one George Fowler and he was with him for years, George lived near so he took him to work in the van.

They got some tricky jobs. One was installing photographic equipment in. The drawings (blue prints) were too large in the production departments. So were damaged a lot. They had a large place to keep them in. But there was a fire risk and in a fire all the drawings could have been lost. So photos were taken of them. They were reduced in size so when anyone had a drawing it was only small like a clock card. On the benches there was a machine like a T.V. set, where you put the card in and could move the picture about to whichever part you wanted to see. The cards (drawings) were kept in fireproof cabinets, which would hold hundreds and a lot of space was saved.

The A.E.I. had a big notice at the end of B aisle where people from all over the world came to order steam turbines and generator sets of power stations. On it was written "These steam turbine and generator sets, when started up, have to run for two years nonstop without any attention." Even a Rolls Royce can't do that. Working there was an experience. Something else they had to impress visitors was in the high voltage lab. They had three alloy balls about three ft diameter, one hung up in the roof, the other two near the floor wide apart from each other. People were stood well clear at the back. Then a million volts were sent from one ball to the others. It was like lightning going from one to the others continually. It was heavy work at times, but Norman enjoyed working there and he was there for seven and a half years. Then one day they were asking for volunteers for redundancy. Norman thought "I am getting older and I don't want to be here till I am 65 so I'll volunteer," which he did. One other thing happened while he was at the A.E.I. he had been working away from the main works, at Mosely Road. Where they built the Manchester Bombers during the war.

They had a lot of presses which had to be stripped under the Health and Safety Act. Norman was working there and had three machines in bits. It was Sunday, when he got home, Nancy and the children were watching T.V. so he sat down next to Nancy on the settee. Leslie & Margaret were sitting on a black rug near the fire. Norman felt something on his left leg, above his ankle; he lifted his trousers up and pulled his sock down and a jet of blood shot about three ft on to the black rug just missing Margaret & Leslie. Norman put a handkerchief on it, thinking of what to do about it, he didn't realize it was an artery so he waited a few minutes, then looked again and blood shot out so he put a hanky on again, he then told Nancy, and asked her to get a bucket of cold water so he could put his foot in it, he thought it would stop it and he put his foot in the bucket of cold water which turned red in no time. There was a knock at the front door. It was Norman's sister Dora and her husband Harold. They came in and Dora saw the bucket red and said, "what are you doing? you won't stop that, that way, that's an artery." She got a towel and tied it above Norman's knee, then they went to Wythenshawe Hospital in Dora's car. The doctor came to see to him right away. He sprayed Norman's leg with something, which formed a skin and after it was allowed to dry, they removed the towel. He then said," You will have to have an operation." Norman said," how long will that be six months?" the doctor said, "This is an emergency; we will have to get you in as soon as possible, we are thinking it is near Christmas and you can go to work tomorrow, if it happens again, lie down, put your leg up, put two hands on your leg above the knee and press hard, till someone comes to help you". It was about 7pm and they went home, Dora & Harold stayed for an hour, and then they settled down. Norman went to work the next day, thinking, "I hope it doesn't happen again while I am at work, if I lie down with my leg in the air they will wonder what's going on."

Norman was working away from the main works, at Mosely Road, where they built the Manchester Bomber. He had three machines (presses) in bits. The hospital phoned the firm to say they wanted Norman in for an operation in the morning. Norman's foreman came across to see him and tell him the news and with him was another fitter to carry on with his job. So Norman spent the rest of the day showing the fitter what he was doing and what had to be done. Norman went to the hospital in the morning and was put in a ward and got in bed ready to start the routine. After a lot of questions, tests, and a bath. A doctor stood Norman on a stool while he examined his left leg. Then they shaved all his leg and in his groin, they washed it with some disinfectant and then he was standing on the stool again. A doctor had some blue liquid and a marking pen and he started to mark near Norman's foot and was working his way up his leg, Norman asked him what he was doing? The doctor said," I am marking you where we are going to cut you". He then knocked the bottle over with the blue stuff in and it went all over his foot. Norman said, "you had better get that off, or I will have no foot". He smiled, then washed his foot and got a new bottle and started marking again.

Norman had 50 marks on his leg. After an injection, he was taken to the operating theatre and he was in the annex outside the theatre, waiting to go in. Norman looked at the clock, in front of his trolley. It was 3 30pm. A woman came and said, she was the anaesthetist, she put an injection in the vein on his left hand and he never saw the needle taken out as he was gone. When Norman came round, he was in the same spot in the annex. The clock was 7 30pm so he had been in there four hours and then he was taken back to the ward. They saw he was OK and asked a few questions, then gave him another needle, so he was off to sleep again. Norman woke up next morning it was 9 30am and he felt wide awake, after all that sleep, he had some breakfast. You have got to get out of bed and have a walk to the end of the Ward" which was the other end to where he was so he got out of bed and the blood rushed down inside his leg. The pain made him fall back on to the bed on his back, they said," We know it's painful, but you will have to do it". It took me half an hour to walk there, he walked from bed to bed, each time he put the weight on his left leg it made him stop quick. Norman had 50 cuts, some were small, and the others needed stitches he was in hospital about two weeks and convalesced another two at home.

Then Norman went back to work he was then installing a large broaching machine. It had a platform which the operator had to stand on while working the machine, as it went up and down. So had guardrails on for safety. He put a board on the guardrails on it, like a ship. H.M.S. Neverbudge.

The next big job was a Craven lathe. A new site had to be made for it, as it was going to be made longer. The shaft that was going to be in it would be 140 tons. No one in the world, had ever made one over 90 tons.

So the Gen Men had to find away of joining a shaft in two parts together so that it would stand the strain. Their job was to make the lathe longer. The bed was in two parts, so it had to have another part of bed put in between the existing ones. They each weighed 40tons. They could do the work on the present site. The foundation of the new site when made had to be left for nine months for it to set. So they had two fitters on days and two fitters on nights. Norman was on days and fitted the new bed in, which had to be level and in line. The shafts and lead screws had to be extended. The work was done and the lathe back doing its normal work of 80 and 90 tons shafts.

Norman never saw the 140tons shaft, as he left the A.E.I. before it was sorted out.

CHAPTER 26

Start At Hans Renolds

Norman worked at the A.E.I. for seven and a half years. Then they asked for volunteers for redundancy.

Norman thought, "I am getting older I need to get away from this heavy work." So he volunteered and he was lucky and got another job within a week.

Norman started at Hans Renolds on the Monday after.

Renolds was one of the best firms to work for, best, pay, best conditions, and shortest hours. he worked in a fitting bay. There were about 20 fitters in it. he had my own bench. he was with another fitter for the first week. Old Hans Renolds invented the Roller Chain, he got a knight hood and his sons and grandsons were running the firm after he passed away. Peter, a grandson was one Norman saw most. There was a large house, on top of a hill at the rear of the factory where he used to live. It was built on the Swiss Style, as he was a Swiss engineer. There was rows of houses near the factory that he had built for his workers. He went to live in Cheshire. So gave the large house to his workers, for a social club. In the grounds was fruit trees. He had built a football pitch and cricket pavilion and bowling green, also a car park at the rear of the factory.

The building Norman worked in was separate from the part where they produced the Roller Chain. They made small chain and up to 5" pitch for ferries. They also made chains for hydraulic rammers to ram, one ton shells into the guns, on Royal Navy battle ships.

In the building he worked in, was a fitting bay with overhead Crane, machine shop a tool room, grinding section, tool stores, and tinsmiths with small forge. Norman used to get jobs on the machines in the production building. One day he was returning to his place of work, after doing a job in the production section. Norman had to pass the cricket ground, as he left the building. The Manchester Police used to use the cricket ground. They were playing, so he watched for a few minutes. A man was near him fielding. The ball came for him to catch it and he jumped up, got it, and then dropped it. Norman shouted," butter fingers," All the people watching heard, was looking where that voice came from. The man near Norman knew, he gave him a stern look and he then went back to his place. They had an hour for dinner, so the workers played bowls then.

The old foreman was a good one and new his stuff. He came to Norman one day and said, "I have a small Universal cutter grinder, I have had a few fitters to look at it, but its still not right, I want you to look at it and give it an old fashioned look." Norman went to it, the bearings on the main spindle needed repair, most of all, the belt on the spindle was the wrong one. It was a belt with a metal fastener on. It should have been an endless and rubberized one. Norman sorted it out, as a belt with a fastener on, transmits the knocking of the fastener, on to the job and he did the bearings, then the job was done. The foreman was delighted with it. He said, "will you have an apprentice with me?" Norman said, "I don't mind." So the first one he worked with was messing about, started leaving the job, he didn't pay attention and had his mates coming for a chat. So Norman told him off and he said, "I don't have to have you, if you don't toe the line, I will get rid of you. I don't know it all, but I will teach you all I know." He was OK after that. So everyone Norman had after that, he read the riot act to them right away. Two out of twelve, were first class, would make good fitters. Norman had them for different times and different ages. The old foreman retired. The new one was a lot younger that he was. One day he came to Norman's bench, and said, "What's all this rubbish on your bench? Get it cleared up." Norman said, "This is a work bench, not an office desk. Don't you want me to do any work? As I won't be able to, if I get rid of all that, it's not rubbish, its important, every bit of it". He then changed his mind.

Norman was getting fed up with him. He would give him a job, then take him off it. Before he had finished it. So Norman told him, he was not having this lark and that stopped it.

One day Norman went to his desk (He had to get a note for anything he wanted from the stores) and he said, "What do you want ?" Norman said, "A ball of string," He said, "What do you want a ball of string for?" Norman said, "To tie the machines up, the way you want me to do them." "You're a cheeky beggar you". Norman said, "Away you go." So after that he kept away from Norman.

Old Hans — Renold was a very independent person. He wouldn't join the Masters Federation, so they put pressure on him by not letting him have any steel. He bought it from Germany and America and built his own machines, special purpose ones. He also had his own water. He had a bore hole and needed a lot of water to clean parts. When there was a water shortage, he supplied Manchester with water.

One day a Friday Norman was going to work in his V.W Beetle left-hand drive. As he came to a crossing on Kingsway there was a car in front of him and the lights were on green so he expected the car in front to go through. As the lights changed to amber, the car in front stopped. The road was icy and Norman skidded and hit the car in front, he was angry, it was a woman driver, he said, "What did you stop for? I was going through. You don't stop on amber in that position." She didn't say a word. Norman managed to get to work in the car and then had to get it repaired. It was a real Hitler car, Norman's son in law brought it in Germany while he was in the Army. He drove it all the way to Manchester for Norman. It loved the winter and started first time every morning. The people in Longcroft Grove where Norman lived couldn't get their cars started. They asked Norman why it was, he said," I look after mine, you don't." Norman had a few words with the foreman at Renolds one day. The next week he decided to leave, so he gave the foreman a week's notice, he told him it wasn't over us having words, and he just needed a change. The charge hand said to Norman, "The foreman is very upset at you leaving, he feels he has failed in his foremanship loosing you."

CHAPTER 27

Start At Parkinson - Cowans

So Norman's next job was at Parkinson - Cowan on Talbot Road, he was on the staff there, he was doing the presses under the Health & Safety Act. The firm paid for Norman to go to college to learn about it he had to do the insurance sheets on each machine. An insurance man visited two or three times a year. When he came he had to strip parts of presses, so he could inspect them, he worked on other machines as well as presses. After he had been there over a year, the foreman retired. An electrician, who was also the shop steward, was made foreman. Norman then took the shop stewards job on again. There was four on the team and Norman, an electrician, a man out of the tool room and the convener who was an inspector. The skilled men were on the staff had a working week of thirty seven and a half hours, the rest of the factory were on forty hours. So the skilled men were needed to work the two and a half hours, for which they earned £3 10 s. They agreed to that, to get staff status, it was not their hourly rate, or overtime rate.

This continued for a number of years till the annual wage review one day, the firm would not move on the £3 50s matter. The skilled men said. "We want our hourly rate for The two and a half hours, we are not asking for overtime rate for it, which we are entitled to". The firm would still not move on it. So the skilled men said, "We are working thirty seven and a half hours from now on". So they went in work each day half an hour late which made it thirty seven and a half hours the rest of the factory went to work as normal. But the plant couldn't run without the skilled men. This went on for two weeks. Then the firm suspended Norman and the convener on pay for two weeks. This didn't have any effect. So they got suspended for two weeks without pay.

Then they sacked them both. All the skilled men went on strike and the Unions came in. The district organiser went to see the manager. He came out again and they both went into a room with him. He said to Norman, "You can have your job back", He said to the convener. "You can't", Norman said, "We are both either in or out."

The organiser went back to the manager, and then came back to them. The second offer was, the convener could have his job back, and Norman couldn't. They were trying to split them up, as together they were a good team.

So A.C.A.S. came into it and it had to go to a tribunal. There were three on the board, a retired union man, a retired management man, and a retired barrister in the chair.

The District Organiser (Union) spoke first, he went over the case from start to finish. The chairman asked a few questions. Then the works manager had his turn. The chairman asked him questions also. Then they went out of the room for half an hour. When they came back. The chairman said," this case will have to go to a "full tribunal" for wrongful dismissal, for" "Trade Union Activities". The management knew then, they couldn't win the case. So they went home. Then A.C.A.S. the unions and management had to sort it out between them.

Right in the middle of the strike, which lasted six weeks. Parkinson Cowan had been taken over by the Thorn Group, so they were overseeing matters.

During the strike the workers, other than the skilled ones, were in the factory, at first doing nothing, but getting paid. Then they were laid off without pay. The firm then started offering Norman and the convener money. They knew then they would not get their jobs back, if they did, they would be marked men. Anything out of line and they would be sacked. So they had to push it, of money as high as they could get. It got to £15,000, £7,500 each. An agreement was drawn up, by all parties and signed by A.C.A.S., Unions, management, and the convener and Norman. On it was a good character reference for them both, so they could get another job. They both had no copy of the agreement. When they got the cheques and money due to them plus holiday pay. The cheques were wrong. Norman's was £7, 000 and the convener £8,000.

Norman said to the convener, "I am not having this", He said, "we don't want to go in there again. We can sort it out ourselves. All we have to do is go to a bank now, pay the cheques in, then as soon as they are cleared and he will give you a cheque for £500". He didn't have a car so Norman took him home and to the factory during the strike. The convener lived in Salford and Norman lived in Wythenshawe. He never gave Norman petrol money and it was about six or seven miles away. When the time came to go to the bank to get Norman's £500, the convener said," I am not going to give you the £500, you don't need it as much as me, you have a house". Norman said, "That's got nothing to do with the matter, it's what the agreement is. Norman was very angry and on the verge of thumping him. Norman said to himself. "Count to ten, think, and don't lose your temper." Norman then said. "You are not going to get away with this I will fight you all the way". Norman got in his car and went home and went to town to see A.C.A. When he got there, the man who was dealing with the case came to him and said, "Hallo Mr Moors, what are you doing here?" Norman said, "I need the agreement". He didn't ask why. He said, "Wait a minute, and I'll get a few photostats". He came back and gave Norman the original one so he went home and Nancy was delighted. After a long talk with Nancy we had always dreamed and planned to retire and live in Blackpool. They lived in a council house, which Norman had bought. So he got the children together and told them he was going to sell the house, and buy one in Blackpool. It would be a two bed roomed one, as Margaret was still at home. He wanted to give her some happiness. Leslie was happy about it, he said, "Blackpool here we come". When they were children and Norman took them to Wales or anywhere else. Leslie would say, "When are we having a holiday dad?" he would say, "You have just had one." "O that's not a holiday; we want to go to Blackpool", Being on a maintenance department, he could always, split his holidays, as firms wanted them to work shutdown. So he took the family to Blackpool for a week.

The next step was to put the house up for sale and to go to see a solicitor up town in Manchester. Norman told him he wanted him to deal with the sale of a House in Manchester and buy one in Blackpool.

Also he had a private matter he wanted him to deal with. They talked about the house first. Then the solicitor said," what's this private matter?" Norman told him and gave him the agreement. He read it, and then said, "You have no chance. It will cost you more than £500, if this matter goes to court". Norman said," he is a difficult person and he will take it to the line". "Well we will send him a letter first", he said.

All this was reported in the Manchester Evening News. When Norman went to his union branch, which was at the Brooklands Labour Club. Everyone was talking about it. The secretary of the branch told Norman that the Union District Office knew about the convener doing the nasty trick on him and the Parkinson Cowan firm being the cause of it. So they would put pressure on him to pay Norman the £500.

In the meantime, Norman was busy sorting things out for moving, he made a few trips with Nancy to Blackpool, looking at houses.

It took a while before the pressure on the convener took effect. Then one day Norman got a cheque for £500 and he told the solicitor. So then they proceeded with selling the house. Norman told the Estate Agent, he was lowering the price. So very soon, they got a buyer. Norman then went house hunting in Blackpool. The brother of the man he worked with at Massey Harris's who played the piano, Harry Prax lived in Blackpool and Norman knew him as he worked at Renolds.

Harry Prax was in the Navy as a Wireless Telegraphist. So Norman went with Nancy to see him and his wife. They helped them find a house. The one they found was a two bedroom mid-Terraced house in Camden Road, Layton and Nancy liked it and the price was OK. Norman bought it. There was a lot of work to be done to get it to their liking. They received a grant off the council. In the V, W. Beetle he took all the seats out, except the driver's seat and he put a lot of stuff on the floor. Then set off to Blackpool one Sunday morning at 6 am and stayed for a week working on the house, so that they could move in.

CHAPTER 28

Off To Blackpool

It was January 1980 and the house needed some form of heating. Norman took the fireplace out and had the chimney swept. Then he made a new concrete hearth and bought a wooden fire surround, and a five bar gas fire. Then he got a plumber in to fit a wall mounted boiler in the kitchen and full central heating. All lead piping out and copper pipes fitted. Norman went home to get Nancy. Margaret didn't want to go to Blackpool. So went to stay with Edith in West Sussex. At first they used the front bedroom to sleep in and Norman used the back bedroom as a workplace. Nancy used to go next door to stay with Florrie, a lady who was on her own, while Norman got on with all the work. he mostly worked in the mornings as Nancy wanted to go out for dinner, with the place being in a mess. Nancy wanted Norman to take her to Manchester very often, so the work was going to take a long time. Norman had to make the hatch into the loft bigger, so they could have a plastic water tank in the loft three ft round and a small one for the central heating in the loft. The loft was a right mess and it had never been cleaned since the place was built, bird's nests and bricks needed renewing on each side, mostly the ones supporting the main roof beam. First he cleaned the loft out and it took him a week, he was coming out of it, as if he had been down the mine (all black). Norman then put insulation between the joist, and put block board over most of the loft, for the tanks to rest on. That also was needed for a support for the main roof beam. While he renewed the bricks which were perished, he had to do one end at a time. There were about 40 bricks in the dividing wall, but he could only replace two, three or four at a time. Norman had to Drill them loose, without using a hammer. So it took him months. The rest was a new front door, new windows, living room and kitchen and the roof recovered, rewired. Norman fitted a new kitchen and did the living room, bedrooms and the bathroom, himself. Norman built a shed and made a back yard door, he worked on the car, many other things. It took two years, it was a good job he got a grant. It was now time to enjoy Blackpool. Norman changed the left-hand V.W. Beetle, for a right-hand drive Beetle. It wasn't as good as the left-hand drive. Norman didn't have it long, when he part exchanged it at a dealers, for a Talbot Horizon, he had it a day or two, then found it had a faulty gear change, so he took it back. They said, "Nothing wrong with it." Norman insisted, so their mechanic drove it, with him to his home, as they were going to see to it. They were near his home, when it jumped out of gear, "your right ", said the mechanic. "It is faulty". So next day Norman went to see them. They said, "Take your pick; you can have any car you like". he picked a Ford Escort at no extra charge. Norman took it to the main dealer for an M.O.T., even though it wasn't due for one. They said it needed a new shock absorber. So he took it back to the dealer, who had to put it right. Norman had the car for a few years with no trouble. Then he sold it to his son cheaply, so he was without a car for a while and then he got a Ford Fiesta a five door Hatchback. Norman had that a few years. One day he was on his way home and got to the Plymouth roundabout, and was on it in the left-hand lane, there were cars in front of him and at the right side of him and behind him. Norman couldn't believe it, and someone tried to enter the round about and was going to hit him, he tried to turn away from him, but couldn't as there was no room. He hit him at the near side front and he braked, and then pulled into the side road.

Norman was very angry and he took his address and all his particulars and went home. Next day Norman went to see him. The address the driver had given him was an empty house. Norman asked the people next door and they gave Norman the address he had moved to so he went to see the police but they weren't interested. Norman finally got him and sorted it out. Norman had the car for a while after it was repaired. Norman's granddaughter Deborah was out of work, then got a job, so she needed a car, so Norman said, "you can have mine, "So she came from Buckinghamshire with her mum to Blackpool and they drove it home. So Norman had no car for a few years.

CHAPTER 29

Gall-Bladder Operation

All was going well, till one night about 1 pm Norman had developed a very bad pain in the top of his stomach. he didn't wake Nancy and he got up went down stairs, the pain pulled him to the floor, he looked at the clock, and it was just after 1 pm. No matter what he did, he couldn't get relief. It lasted two hours severe, then one hour to go away and he went back to bed. It didn't happen every night. So he didn't tell Nancy. One night he went down stairs with the pain and Nancy woke up, saw he wasn't there and came down stairs and saw Norman in pain. She phoned for a doctor. As there is only one doctor on standby in Blackpool. You have to wait. By the time he came the pain had gone. So he doesn't do anything, as he has other people to see to. Norman went to see his doctor, he examined him and said, "You will have to go to hospital for a scan and you will get a letter." When Norman got a letter and had the scan. The doctor said, "You have got a hiatus hernia, but that is not what is giving you the pain you have got, it's your gall bladder, you have got stones in it and you will have to have an operation, but there is a waiting list." So Norman went home and waited and kept getting the pain. A doctor would come sometimes and give him an injection for the pain. Then one night a doctor came early, when it was at its worse and his skin was yellow. The doctor got an ambulance,

After arriving at Victoria Hospital, Blackpool in the ambulance. Norman was taken to an isolation ward. They did tests on him, blood, temperature, weigh. Norman was then put on a water diet, a small glass full, and every hour, his skin was yellow, also the white of his eyes and this lasted for ten days and then it had gone and he was moved to a surgical ward. In there for a few days and then he shaved and washed ready for the operation.

Which was to remove stones from Norman's gall bladder.

The anaesthetist put an injection in the vein of his left hand, and then he was put to sleep. Norman woke up a few hours later in the ward, a nurses spoke to him to see if he was all right. Then the doctor and the surgeon came to see him, to tell him about the operation. The doctor said Norman's gall bladder was infected, so it had to be removed completely, which was attached to his liver, "Normally we would have just removed the stones, as it is part of your digestive system, you will stay on a water diet for a while and have injections to see if your liver is working all right." In the ward, it was cubicles, two beds in each one. The one Norman was in, he was facing a Scotsman and he was being fed by a drip. When he was able to get up he still had the drip on, it was on a frame with wheels, so he could hold it and walk about the ward, he also had a drain bag with a pipe going to his liver. This lasted for a number of weeks. One day, as they gave the meals out, (Norman had not ordered any) they gave him a dinner. So he thought it was alright, so being hungry he ate it and after a short while he started to feel pain, in the region of the operation, so he was moving about in the bed. The man opposite noticed him, so he shouted for a nurse, one came to him, and so he pointed to Norman, and she came to him then, and asked him what the matter was and he told her he had a pain where the operation had been so she went for a doctor.

A woman doctor came, and to Norman's surprise, she started to tell him off. She said, "We are very busy, there are people in this ward, worse off than you, so what are you shouting about?" Norman said, "Have you finished?" ". "I didn't shout for the nurse, the man opposite shouted for the nurse, as he saw I was in pain, I am not soft I don't call for a nurse unless I need one. If I do, I am in a hospital where you can stick a needle in me to kill the pain, if need be".

I have had surgery to remove the pain, so something must be wrong, now get your facts right, before you start telling people off.

"She calmed down and didn't say sorry. They then found out he should not have had a dinner, so they then were looking for who had sent a dinner for him.

Before Norman went in hospital, there was a cat that used to come on the yard wall, it was a black and white tom cat, and a big one, when Norman went near it, it would spit at him and go away. So he put a saucer of milk in the yard for it, every day. Norman's daughter Margaret came to stay with her mum, while he was in hospital. So she gave the cat the milk. She got the cat to come in the house and called it Spit Moors. So when Norman came out of hospital they had a cat, it had the loudest purr you have ever heard. Margaret and Nancy came to visit him while he was having that trouble over the dinner matter and when Margaret heard about it; she went and told the nursing staff off.

The time came for the drain bag and pipe to be removed. First the bag, then the pipe. he was told to take a deep Breath and when he exhaled they would pull the pipe out a bit at a time. he was laid down on a couch. The bag was no trouble and the pipe took a lot of exhales before it was out. Norman was surprised how big and long it was, when it was out and the nurse said," you can have a rest now, just lay there for a while, would you like some music?"

Norman said, "I will sing to you," she said, "OK, what are you going to sing? "I said, "Maggie May, a sailors song". "I have never heard that ", She said, "OK, Sing it".

Norman sang Maggie May to the nurse, she said," very good, now have a rest for an hour, then you will be taken back to the ward. It was near Christmas 1986 and he was wondering if he could be home by then. Norman spent Christmas in the hospital and came out on New Year's Eve. Margaret was still looking after Nancy and the cat, Spit. Norman had two cans of beer in the fridge, so being New Years Eve. he drank them. After a short while he started being ill, so Margaret phoned the hospital, they sent an ambulance and he was back in the ward. Two doctors came to him and asked him what he had been doing, to make him ill? Norman said," I drunk two cans of beer, I had in the fridge." They said, they didn't think that, that would do any harm and they then moved away from me a few yards and were talking to each other, he was watching them; they had a frown on their faces, a worried look. So that set Norman thinking that the operation had gone wrong. After a short while they came back to him and they said they were going to keep Norman in hospital under observation for a week or more and they said, "No alcohol for the rest of your life and a low fat diet for the rest of your life." Norman was in for ten more days and during that time a dietician came to him and gave him three sheets of diet lists and explained about his digestive system. At first he was on water only for a day, and then they slowly got him onto solids, from the diet sheet. Norman then was back home again. Margaret stayed for a week or more and after she left, they got help from social services to do shopping and cleaning until he was able to do it himself.

CHAPTER 30

Holidays In Scotland

Norman's sister Dora and Harold asked their family to go to Scotland with them for a holiday, for three weeks, touring all over. They said, "Yes". So off they went, first to the Western Isles.

They stayed one night at Ullapool at a bed and breakfast. Then they took the ferry over to Isle of Lewis. The people there were living in huts and the huts were called black houses and they called them crofters. Some were better off as they had caravans. One or two had built a brick houses. They went on to Harris, where they make the Harris Tweed. They went in the factory to see how they made it. They stayed the night on Harris at a B& B, then on to North Uist. There were causeways to go from one Island to another, so they could use the car. North Uist and South Uist had grass on, so they could have cattle and sheep. They took the ferry on to Skye and stayed the night B & B then they returned to the mainland. They toured the Highlands; Loch Ness, Fort William and Loch Awe where H.M.S. Rodney used to hide, during the war waiting for the big German war ships coming from Norway to the Atlantic, to attack the convoys. There was a large area, near Loch Awe which had a lot of plants and flowers from all over the world owing to the warm Gulf Stream current. They didn't get to see them, as they didn't get ashore.

They saw a Russian factory ship with it's own fleet of trawlers fishing in our waters.

They did a lot of travelling, and then it was time to go home. While in Blackpool, they had a lot of visits from family and friends.

The family Edith, Wayne, Darren, Margaret, Leslie, Maureen, William and Charlotte, children and grand children came to see Norman while he was in hospital and afterwards, they went to enjoy Blackpool on the beech and all was fine for a while.

So the family made plans to go to Scotland on the east side, Norman wrote to places in Aberdeen, Dundee, and Edinburgh. They were going for three weeks. A week in each place, Norman wrote 40 letters, they just had to sort out which one for each place. Then Nancy changed her mined and only wanted a week. So they rented a Bungalow for a week in Aberdeen. They went by car. Norman had a Ford Escort 1-3 a, five door hatch back. They visited castles, distilleries, and Balmoral Castle. They went in one distillery and saw a film show, you could put head phones on and pluged in for different languages and a guide for groups of ten each. The guide was dressed in full tartan dress. Each guide with a different tartan. They showed us all round and explained how whisky was made. You could buy whisky, tartan kilts, of different tartans and Scotch woollies. Norman bought Nancy a blue type tartan kilt, Think it was a Portree one and a woolly for Nancy and one for himself. At the end they were given some whisky in a glass. Norman was going to refuse it, as no alcohol for the rest of his life. But there was only a small amount at the bottom of the glass, and he filled it up with water and drank it. They came out and very soon Norman felt ill, Nancy was worried so was Norman as he had to drive the car back to Aberdeen. They sat down wondering what to do, and then he said to Nancy. "Let's go for something to eat, maybe that will help". So they looked for a café and found one and had a good meal. It did the trick and he felt OK again. He never touched alcohol since. They got back to Aberdeen alright and saw a bit of Aberdeen. Then they went to a cinema and had a rest in the bungalow which was very peaceful, the lady who rented it was very friendly, then it was time to go home. They set of early on Saturday morning, The journey was OK till they got to Edinburgh where it was packed with cars. Some were stopping in the middle of the road, then getting out and leaving the car blocking the road. Norman thought he was never going to get out of Edinburgh and he said to Nancy, "that's it; I am using a train next time". They got home OK the cat was very pleased to see them, as the lady next door had been looking after Spit. He never stopped purring and followed them all over the place. He had a big box to sleep in. Norman trained him to get in it and he missed his box at Florries, next door.

CHAPTER 31

Norman Saw Ghosts

Norman was lying awake in the back bedroom at 16, Camden Road, Layton, Blackpool. It was about four am he heard a slight wind, then a full body of George Whitingham was standing at the bedroom door, he was about 6ft tall, he thought it's George Whitingham, but he was only 5ft 6in or Ten, the last time he had seen him. He had died of cancer a few years ago, he was with him the day he died. He was gone within a minute, then another one appeared, just head and shoulders this was a man about 50 dark hair and slightly bald and Norman didn't recognize him at that time but may have been his father. Then others came, one had a three cornered hat on, there was ten in all, the last one was a very old man, with long tufts of hair hanging, Norman had never seen anyone so old, he was ancient. He waited for half an hour but no more came and he was expecting a message, but none came and he was so disappointed. Norman spoke to the Priest at St Kentigern's Church about it. He said that the message was that there is life after death and those were your ancestors and they are their spirits conveying the message to you.

Since then Norman had seen his wife Nancy in the flat, 81 Argosy Avenue, Grange Park, Blackpool, twice. She died on March 19th 1989 of cancer.

A lot of things have happened since then, he was at St Kentigern's Church for many years and he took confirmation classes to become a Catholic.

George Whitingham was Norman's brother in law and they got on well together. Norman liked him the very moment he met him. George was married to Leah, Nancy's sister. After Nancy died, Norman was living on his own at 16 Camden Road. Layton, Blackpool.

Norman found he couldn't sleep in a double bed and was cold on his own. he tried electric blanket and he was too hot. So Norman started to sleep down stairs in the living room, on a bed settee, he made a sleeping bag, which did the trick and he slept great, The only trouble, was he had to go to the toilet in the night upstairs and had a few slight falls down the stairs because the stairs were not a full stair but were narrow and steep making matters worse. Norman thought about a stairlift and got a firm who sold them to come and see the stairs. Because they had a sharp turn at the start, they said they didn't make a stair lift that turned corners, so that was no use.

Norman thought about doing away with the stairs altogether. Which would make the pantry larger, as the stairs went across it, that would mean removing some of the stairs at the start and having a lift to go up and down to upstairs level. Then all the stairs could be removed and a long landing could go from the lift to the upstairs landing. Norman got a lift firm in to see the job. They weren't very keen, on what he told them what he wanted. They said, it would cost a few thousand pounds, to do it. There were Safety Regulations to contend with. Norman got the message, they didn't want the job.

Then Norman had a big fall from top of the stairs and caved his right ribs in, on the bottom stair, he lay there on his own, thinking he had better watch what he does when he moves, as he knew he had done some damage to himself. After about ten minutes he made his way carefully to the phone in the living room and phoned his doctor. He came and took me to Victoria Hospital, Blackpool. Accident Department. The doctor waited a while, then they examined Norman, it was a young doctor, he said, "I am discharging you, I want you to go home and take deep breathing exercises, it will be painful, but gradually it will let your ribs right themselves". Norman couldn't believe what he was saying. So Norman said," you must be joking" He said, "I am not, that's all I can do for you". So reluctantly he went home. Norman's ribs slowly corrected themselves with a lot of painful deep breathing exercises. But are still caved in, compared with his left one.

CHAPTER 32

Moving House

So Norman made up his mind to leave 16 Camden Road and he went to see the Housing Dept and they gave him a list of council flats, sheltered accommodation. In different areas in Blackpool. he went to see them all. Some were bad area and there was no way would he live there. Norman finally picked one on Argosy Avenue, on the outskirts of Grange Park, near the football pitches of Boundary Park. Norman phoned his eldest daughter Edith, she came to see him at the Flat, which was in a block of nine Flats, three floors, and three flats on each floor and bottom ones sheltered, with alarms and a warden. She said, she would borrow her firms big van, on a Saturday. Norman's grandson, Wayne the eldest drove it to move Norman into his flat. When he got the OK from the Housing and moved into the Flat on 12th August 1996. It took two trips with the big van. Wayne also moved the delicate stuff with his car, a Ford Fiesta 1-3 Hatch Back five doors, and a few trips.

Norman's son Leslie was on his holidays at the time, for a fortnight. he had a lot of work to do in the Flat.

The heating was hot air, which he had never had before, but being a maintenance fitter in engineering, he had some had dealings with things of this nature. Norman thought, that as he had to breathe that air in, he'd better check it. He removed the grill near the floor in the living room, where the hot air came out. It was full of fluffy stuff, so he removed all lower grills, one in the hall, one in the bedroom, they were all the same, full of fluffy stuff, and it was metal trunking. So he cleaned it all out, there was builders rubbish in it also. He got the vac and cleaned the trunking out spotless. It had not been cleaned since the place had been built in 1970. As it was August he didn't need the heating. The hot water was by immersion heater. So he got on with all the other things he had to do. Norman's son came back from his holidays. He phoned Norman and asked what heating was in the flat.

Norman told him hot air. Leslie said he was taking them out in Manchester (he was a plumber and heating engineer) as two people had died with fumes entering their homes. The Environmental Health had said that all those hot air systems had to be out, by the year 2000. He said, "Don't use it dad, and get it checked. Norman told him about the fluffy stuff. he then got in touch with the Housing Dept and they sent a man from British Gas.

Who checked it with a smoke block. Norman told him and the Council, "I am not using this system till it is checked properly. They got rid of British Gas, who had the Contract and got a firm from Liverpool. A man from the Council watched them check it, Norman also watched. The Council man said, to the Liverpool man, "You don't know what you are doing". They got fired out. Then they got a Blackpool firm.

Reed Errington. he watched them check it, they had proper things to use. They said, "fumes are entering this flat. They found the flue blocked and broken. Also it was asbestos. They had to get on the roof.

In the meantime he needed the heating. The Council Said, "You can have central heating, but you will have to pay for it yourself." He had to buy two electric oil filled radiators (mobile ones) to keep warm that winter. Then he bought a central heating system. Norman's son installed it in for him. Norman drilled all the holes in the walls for the pipes and put the radiators on the walls before he came.

Later the Council took all the hot air systems out and put gas central heating in the houses.

When he leave this flat the Council has promised to compensate him for all the work and expense he has had and done. If Norman dies his next of kin will get it. All the work took Norman two years, as he had to do everything himself. Norman was 72 years 8 months when he moved into the flat and he still went to St Kentigern's Church for the first two or three years. Then he went to Christ the King, which was nearer.

It was fairly quiet for a few years, then things started to get troublesome. There was knocking on the bedroom window at two, three and four in the early mornings on a Friday & Saturday.

The people who were doing this had presumably been to late night clubs getting drunk, and perhaps on drugs as well. They smashed new bus shelters, or anything they can find to damage such as cars. December 4th 2007 was Norman's 85th Birthday and he had his kitchen window smashed and the next night his living room window was smashed. The flat above me, had it's kitchen window smashed and that also happened to a flat (sheltered) behind him. These crimes were done in the early evenings.

CHAPTER 33

Trade Unionism

Norman first joined the A.E.U.(Amal Gamated Engineering Union) in 1946 when he came out of the Royal Navy. Norman had broken his seven years apprenticeship, so he was three years short. He joined Royal Navy on his 18th Birthday. The Union took into account what he had been doing while he was in the Navy. They said, he would have to do nine months at an engineering firm learning fitting. Then he would be qualified, and be a section one member as a skilled man.

Norman got a job at Locket and Crosslands doing fitting and was there for nine months. The firm paid half his wages, the government the other half. Norman then got his section one card, qualified as a skilled man and he could go anywhere, which he did.

Norman first became a shop steward, at Massey Harrises in 1953. It's was no easy job because you were a marked man and you had to watch your step and keep your nose clean. It was necessary to fight for better wages and conditions and justice at all times. Many men you helped stabbed you in the back. Other firms that he was shop steward at, A.E.I. called the big House. Trafford Park, Manchester and Parkinson and Cowan, Stretford. The men years ago who fought for justice, like The Tolpuddle Martyr's in Dorchester who were transported to Sydney, Australia. That was the start of the Trade Union Movement that grew into the Labour Party of today. Members if you can call them members, want all the benefits the Union has fought to get for them yet they don't pay their dues, don't go to branch meetings. They are too lazy to vote and then they wonder why things are being lost, even our forefathers won when it was very hard to get anything. Things will get worse not better if people don't shape up.

CHAPTER 34

Politics

Democracy, we haven't got it and we have never had it. Democracy is a government in power voted by the majority of people. That means vote right or left with two parties at the final vote. All these other parties are splitting the vote and they shouldn't be. All that means is, a party gets in power and the majority of people didn't vote for it, and it's policy. So when are we going to wake up? America has democracy. Democrats or Republicans.

When are we going to have I.D. cards to help catch the criminals and people in our country illegally? Deport them. Stop anymore coming in, living off the State, we have too many of our own doing that. Unemployment makes it worse.

We need a clean power, not nuclear that is dangerous. It takes two years to shut a nuclear power station to shut down. Dam the Rivers, (Dam the Sea, tides, two ways Dam) Direction of Labour.

We had it in war time, why not peace time? All these foreign cars, Where are ours? Electric cars, Electric monorails in cities. All these things get full employment. Build factories, so children have places to learn a trade. We did it in war time so why not now? Too many imports and not enough exports. We haven't recovered from the damage Thatcher did. She did more damage to this country than Hitler did. Factories not casinos, Crime, if you don't give people a place to earn a living, then they will turn to Crime to get it

Thatcher closed the coal mines, had a big and long strike. She said, "uneconomical pits."

Nonsense! The coal mines had pit ponies pulling trucks, for years. Then the Labour Party put Machines down the mines. Then the coal came out on a conveyor belt, it poured out. It was used in the Power Stations, on Ships, trains, anywhere which needed steam, in the home on the kitchen range, which kept people warm, cooked the food in the oven, boiled the water, dried the clothes. No way can you call that uneconomical. By closing the mines, she put thousands out of work and this broke up many communities and left the people in poverty. All that, after the miners had worked hard, under bad conditions and dangerous.

Many lost their sons and fathers down the mines. Others had their health ruined. Now we import coal from Poland and other countries. While our pits are flooded and millions of pounds worth of machines and equipment are lost. Then they talk of giving her a state funeral.

Things we have lost which we used to make, they now import them, Raleigh, Rudge, Whitworths, New hudson, Hercules, to name a few bicycles, some had three speed hubs, on back wheels. Now we import bikes, Motor Bikes, Norton, Triumph some with two stroke engines. Motor cars, the Electric cars. singer sewing machines, have gone abroad. Insurance companies, took work abroad for cheap labour and put this country on a war footing, a war against poverty and unemployment. Ship building where is it? The Q.E. was built in France. They have recovered better than us and France has been a battle field in two wars. There are plenty of their cars here. Engineering was the back bone of this country. Fishing, Fleetwood, Grimsby, Hull, Aberdeen, where has it gone? Norman saw a large Russian factory ship with a fleet of trawlers, fishing in our waters when he went to Scotland on a holiday.

MPs. and GOVERNMENTS, WAKE UP.

CHAPTER 35

Religion

Norman was brought up as a Methodist and he went to church and Sunday School at Albert Hall in Peter Street, Manchester and later in Tatton Street Mission in Hulme District of Manchester. He was in the Boys Brigade from age 11 to 16, (9th Manchesters) then he changed to Church of England when he joined the Royal Navy on his 18th Birthday and the reason being most of the group was Church of England, so he didn't want to be the odd one out. He stayed there untill he became a Catholic. Norman was Confirmation on April 3rd 1992. At St Kentigerns Church, Blackpool.

What he sees today 2009, in churches they have closed and some have become warehouses and some of the congregation is very small and getting smaller. There are not many with Boys Brigade or Girl Guides. Very few Scouts. Children need to be part of something and to have somewhere to go and some interesting place of activity. Guidance from parents Is needed and we need more schools and parents teaching the Christian way of life, with firmness and discipline, showing love and understanding. All these people coming to our country bringing other religious, has caused a lot of trouble. We have enough trouble of our own, without adding more. Matters that affect a nation in a big way, call for a referendum. It is not for a small group of people like a Cabinet to take a big step that affects everyone. Building mosques, the people weren't asked about that. The African people that come to our country, mix well, and take our religion, so British people accept them better. These things should have been sorted out the start. We have a lot of nonsense going on at the House of Commons. MPs squabble with each other. Their job is to sort things out for the best, for everyone, not this party nonsense which opposes things which are good for the country. They are like children when they are in power. It's like a soap opera.

Sister Grace and Niece Jean (Catherine)

Norman's sister's first name is Grace. She was never called Grace always her second name Edna, like his name being Leslie, got called Norman.

Norman first met his niece Jean at his sister's Cottage in Arley Cheshire. Dora and Husband Harold lived there most of their lives. Nancy and he used to visit them very often. This day we went and found Jean and David there, it was the first time we had seen them, before they got married. Nancy and he were pleased to see them, we stayed a while, then went home.

The time came for Jean and David to get married, as she had never seen her Father, as he went away as soon as he knew her mother Grace was pregnant, never to be seen again. So Jean needed someone to give her away. When asked he said, "Yes, I'll do it". So he gave her away at the Wedding to David Huntridge On August 2nd 1975. Norman gave a speech at the Wedding Reception about equality, caring and sharing the bad times as well as the good.

After her mothers' funeral, Norman took Jean on a holiday to Lourdes, a pilgrimage. Then she moved to Sale, Manchester.

Norma had to sort out a head stone for Grace Edna's grave and they had put on the grave stone.

"HEARTS ARE BROKEN OF GREAT LOSS BUT WILL REUNITE BEFORE THE CROSS".

CHAPTER 36

Catherine's Testimony To Norman

One day Norman's niece Catherine sat with him in the Catholic Social Club in Blackpool over a non- alcoholic larger for him and Catherine had a Guinness and she told him her testimony which had a powerful effect on him

This is what Catherine told him:-

WHEN I MET OUR LADY

My name was Jean when I was a child. I was fourteen and attending senior school and one day after school my foster mother said,

"You can go and visit your real mother". I said, "No I can't, she is dead." My foster mother said,

"No she is not, she survived the car accident when you were two and we have traced her, the Childcare officer will take you to see her."

I was so excited and full of expectation of a new life with my real loving mother.

So the day came at the office and this strange woman came shouting crazy things.

I thought she must be from a mental home. I was so devastated and heartbroken; I stormed out

The room shouting, "That's not my mother." It took me weeks to get over the shock and disappointment and the relationship between my foster mother and I became much worse.

One evening on the way home from school I had a panic attack during which I questioned my life and I asked God. “Why am I here? Who am I? and where did I come from? Who do I belong to? And where am I going in life? I was afraid of my own existence and my surroundings and I felt Overwhelmed by my circumstances.

When I arrived at the park there were no children in the playground.

I walked round a roundabout a few times until I grew tired and dizzy so I lay down on the grass.

It was starting to get dark, so I decided to go home. My foster mother shouted. “What time do call this? You’ve missed your tea.” I said, “I needed to go for a walk.” I couldn’t tell her what was Going on and how I felt so I went to bed and I read a book called “Great Expectations” for a while, Then I fell asleep.

I soon found myself in a nightmare. I was dreaming that my foster parents and foster brothers and I were walking round a lake and then my foster family drowned and I was drowning, suddenly I was in a panic, this is it, I am going to die I thought, and I struggled to wake up, then I awoke startled.

I sat up in bed and pinched myself to make sure I was still alive and awake.

The moon was shining through my window next to my bed.

I noticed my travel alarm on the floor as if someone had placed it there. It was not closed and the time said 12.00. Then I saw a brilliant light shine from the window, it soon filled my room.

I felt scared, but in awe as I saw a figure appearing. I thought, maybe it’s an angel.

I saw she had a veil covering her golden brown hair. She was wearing a radiant white dress and she had a blue robe round her. I saw she had bell sleeves as she raise her arms and smiled with her compassionate bright blue eyes of love.

In a soft gentle voice she said, “You are a child of God and I am you mother.”

My heart melted as I felt her love and I longed for this moment to last for ever.

Then she said, “I am the mother of Jesus, listen to my Son.”

And I heard a loud voice saying, "Do not be afraid, for I am always with you."

I turned around to try to find Jesus, but to no avail, the brilliant light faded, then Mary (Our Lady) had gone.

I was awestruck and so excited by what I'd seen and heard. I could not sleep till the early hours of the morning. At 6 am. I thought, it's Friday, I've got to get up for school I an hour, and I'd better go to sleep. When I did, I went back into the nightmare of drowning. In the dream Mary (Our Lady) came and saved me; She brought me past a large tree to a table in a sunny garden, where the twelve disciples were sitting. There was a chair at the end of the table, so I sat there, thinking I know my place at the bottom, but Mary took me by the hand and brought me to the top of the table to meet Jesus and I sat next to him.

He smiled and gave me some bread and said, "This is my body, eat from me," and then he gave me a gold chalice of wine and said, "This is my blood, drink from me for I am always with you."

He hugged me tight and I could feel his warmth and amazing love.

Then I woke up elated, awestruck and excited. When I got up I noticed that my chair had been moved from up against the wall next to my bed round to the side of my bed to face me and I remembered it was placed like that just before I saw the vision of Mary sitting on the chair.

I heard her soft voice say, "My Son is a perfect gentleman" I thought Jesus had moved the alarm clock and the chair ready for his mother's visit. I heard her soft voice say, "Yes, my dear, So you may know I draw people to Jesus my Son."

I felt Jesus's strong presence with me and I felt comforted.

I was thinking how awesome, and that the Lord had answered all five questions.

1. I am here because the Lord put me here to do his will.
2. I came from God.
3. I am a child of God.
4. I belong to God and our Lord Jesus Christ.
5. I am going where ever the Lord Jesus leads me.

Finally I realised I have received a great light in my darkness.

The next day at school my best friend Sarah said, "Why have you been falling asleep all day?"

I said, "I've been awake all night because I had a vision," Sarah said, "Tell me about it"

And another friend Hannah, who was with us said, "Its P.E. this afternoon and its cross country running. We could take a detour and go to my house as it's only ten minutes away."

So we went to Hannah's house and her mum gave us tea and cakes and I told them all that had happened during the night and they were awestruck and amazed.

Hannah's mum, Esther, said, "In my church, the Catholic Church, we call the mother of Jesus Our Lady. In 1858 Our Lady appeared several times to Bernadette in Lourdes, South of France.

Bernadette was told to dig a well and when she obeyed a spring of water appeared and as people gathered round her many miracles took place. Bernadette was very special and years after she died, She became a saint.

People from all over the world came to Lourdes for healing. There is a grotto where our Lady appeared and churches were built around it.

Today it is a famous place for pilgrims to worship and receive healing, peace and renewed strength And spiritual growth.

In the Bible Mary the Mother of Jesus is said to be very special and in the New Testament there is a Song about her, called the Magnification. Esther read it out.

MARY'S SONG THE MAGNIFICATION

"My soul doth magnify the Lord and my spirit hath rejoiced in God my Saviour, for he hath regarded the low estate of his handmaiden, for behold from henceforth all generations shall call me blessed.

For he that is mighty hath done great things and Holy is his name.

His mercy is on those that fear him from generation to generation.

He hath showed strength with his arm, he hath scattered the proud in the imagination of their hearts.

He hath put down the mighty from their seats and exalted those of low degree. He hath filled the hungry with good things and the rich he hath sent empty away. He hath helped his servant Israel In remembrance of his mercy.

As he spoke to our fathers, to Abraham and to his seed forever.

Xxxxxxxxxxxxxxxxxxxx

When Esther had finished reading to us I said, "How awesome, imagine being with Jesus for thirty three years and being so close, caring and serving him. The disciples only had three years with him;

I wish I could meet him" (Little did I know that in a few years' time my wish would come true) Esther said, "Well Jean it's so awesome and unusual for you to see Our Lady like you did last night as very few people do see her. You are very Blessed."

I found it so awesome that I had been told by Mary, Jesus's Mother that I'm a child of the Almighty God which means I belong to God and his family. I felt our Lord's presence and I felt greatly comforted by the knowledge that I finally belong to somebody, to the Almighty God and Jesus Christ my Saviour. I was filled with such love and awe that I had ever known before.

WHEN I MET OUR LORD

By the time I was seventeen, on 21st July 1971, life had become unbearable;

I was in so much turmoil and pain, that I went to my bedroom while the family were all having tea downstairs. I was so depressed and overwhelmed by my suffering, I took two full bottles of tablets, one bottle of Valuim and the other barbiturates with a glass of water, and I opened the sash window. I sat on the window sill and looked up at the sunshine in the blue sky. I cried out to God and said,

"God if you love me, save me now." I felt very dizzy from the tablets and then I jumped from the bedroom window. At the hospital I was told later that I had been unconscious for three days before my heart failed and stopped on the 23rd July 1971.

The next thing I knew, I found my spirit on the hospital ceiling by the lights. Then I saw the doctors and nurses rushing around trying to revive me with heart electric pads. I shouted,

"Don't stop, I can't get back in my body if you do." All failed and they gave up and doctor said,

"It's no good, it's too late, she's gone." As he put the sheet over my face he said, "What a shame, such a waste of life, a pretty young girl, she must have suffered a lot to come to this!"

As I watched from above I said, "Sorry God I didn't mean to end it all, it was a cry for help."

As soon as I said that, suddenly I was going full speed down a tunnel and I felt safe as though God was taking me somewhere, then I came to a light, so bright and dazzling.

I arrived at a beautiful garden rich in colour with fresh grass, flowers, trees and streams.

There were clear golden roads leading to mansions in the distance and there were fields and gardens where young people were talking and children were playing, whilst all around angels were flying. It was paradise and the sound of music was everywhere with a complete sense of peace and love.

Then there came a bright light and Jesus appeared. His garments were radiant and white.

The love from his eyes melted my heart as I met Jesus face to face, his presence and his love were so warm and comforting and his voice was gentle but strong and authoritive.

He was so awesome and I was overwhelmed with joy as he held my hands, smiled and lovingly said, "It's not your time yet, I have work for you to do, but I cannot promise you will be free from pain. You have a choice." In the light of his countenance I could not refuse him; there was no room for questioning or doubt. He showed compelling, compassionate love and full acceptance of me. It was awesome.

I looked into Jesus's wonderful face. There was so much love, warmth and light coming from him that I had never known before, it was so amazing and awesome. I thought, I don't want to go back, but I can't say "no" to Jesus. As I gazed into his eyes, there was so much love coming from him and I said, "Yes Lord whatever you say I will do." fully accepting his will.

Suddenly the light faded and I was going full speed down the tunnel, then I found myself staring at the ceiling light, back in the hospital still with the sheet over my face and a tag on my toe.

I pulled the sheet off my face and got up and fell out of bed as I didn't realise my left foot had been broken in the fall. The doctors and nurses looked at me as though they had seen a ghost.

The doctor said, "We had given you up for dead, it's a miracle." I told him all that had happened and he believed me. He told me he had read some stories about near death experiences.

My doctor took into account how unhappy I was at the hostel. He traced Mr and Mrs Ted and Hilda Burney, my aunt and uncle in Middlesbrough, Norman's sister and brother in law and the doctor wrote to them.

To my surprise they accepted me and I was so delighted and relieved that I could go and live with them and from then on my life began to get better and I began a new life with my new family.

I know this Testimony is true as it happened to me, Catherine Jean Mary Hughes.

This story changed Norman's belief system and outlook on life and his niece Catherine helped him to gain confidence in his faith and prayer life and he found peace and Joy in God and Jesus Christ his Saviour.

Norman asked me to write his story so I have written this book in his honour, with him being in the Royal Navy in world war two he has become the Mancunian Hero.

By Catherine J.M. Hughes

Picture of Catherine
Norman Leslie Moors's
Niece.

Printed in Great Britain
by Amazon

79627082R00123